The Stenciled Quilt

Book design by Margo Letourneau
Illustrated by Maryann Mattson

Color photographs by Terry Burton, Traverse City, Michigan

Yankee Publishing Incorporated
Dublin, New Hampshire
First Edition
First Printing, 1986
Copyright 1986 by Yankee Publishing Incorporated

Library of Congress Catalogue Card Number: 86-50090
ISBN: 0-89909-103-2

The Stenciled Quilt

Create your own quilts, pillows,
wall hangings — more than 30 designs with instructions,
plus a portfolio of patterns.

by Marie Monteith Sturmer

YANKEE BOOKS

A division of Yankee Publishing Incorporated
Dublin, New Hampshire

Contents

7 Preface

8 A Whole-Cloth Stenciled Quilt, circa 1820

11 Introduction

14 Part One: The Quilts
The collection of quilts (with color plates)

34 Part Two: The Stencil
Making the Stencil: *Materials. Tracing or Copying. Cutting.*
Preparing to Paint: *Paints. Brushes. Miscellaneous Supplies.*
Painting on Fabric
Stenciling Techniques: *Textures. Colors.*
Designing Original Patterns

42 Part Three: The Making of a Quilt
Planning and Preparing: *Fabric. Batting. Other Supplies.*
Making a Quilt Top: *Cutting Fabric. Patchwork Tops. Appliquéd Whole-Cloth Tops.*
Assembling a Quilt: *Templates. Other Supplies. Basting. Quilting. Tying.*
Finishing a Quilt: *Edges. Corners.*
Caring for a Quilt

50 Instructions, stencil patterns, and templates for the collection of quilts

120 Part Four: The Smaller Project

Guidelines for stenciling canvas tote bags and log carriers, pillows, bibs, upholstery fabric, fireplace screens, floorcloths, floors, and walls

126 Part Five: The Portfolio

Original stencil patterns, including contemporary and Early American border, frieze, medallion, and pieced and appliqué quilt designs

158 Resources

Books
Mail-Order Suppliers

Color Plates

Page
17 Wild Rose (*plate 1*)
18 Sweetheart (*plate 2*)
    Scotch Thistle (*plate 3*)
19 American Tulip (*plate 4*)
    Christmas Star (*plate 5*)
    Country Chickens (*plate 6*)
20 Birds of a Feather (*plate 7*)
21 Whig Rose (*plate 8*)
    Teddy Bear (*plate 9*)

Page
22 Holly Wreath (*plate 10*)
    Running Rabbits (*plate 11*)
    Leaf and Chain (*plate 12*)
23 Victorian Crazy Quilt (*plate 13*)
    Rose Wreath with Tulips (*plate 14*)
24 Turkey Tracks (*plate 15*)
    Song Birds (*plate 16*)
    Rose of Sharon (*plate 17*)
25 Circle of Tulips (*plate 18*)
    Hearts and Flowers (*plate 19*)
    Creeping Periwinkle (*plate 20*)
26 Art Nouveau (*plate 21*)
    Blue Whig Rose (*plate 22*)

Page
27 Dutch Tulips (*plate 23*)
    Hearts and More Hearts (*plate 24*)
    Rose Wreath and Bud (*plate 25*)
28 Christmas Rose of Sharon (*plate 26*)
    Oak Leaf and Reel (*plate 27*)
29 Art Deco (*plate 28*)
30 Laurel Leaf (*plate 29*)
    Peter Rabbit (*plate 30*)
31 Whirl of Maple Leaves (*plate 31*)
    True Oak Leaves (*plate 32*)
    Pineapple (*plate 33*)
32 Theorem Theme (*plate 34*)

To my loving parents, Ellsworth and Bessie Monteith, who encouraged me in all my artistic endeavors, and to my husband, Ralph, for his patient support.

Acknowledgments

I wish to express my deep gratitude to Doris Robinson for sharing her heirloom stenciled quilt with me. The moment she showed me the quilt I knew I had to pursue this craft, reviving the techniques of stencil painting I had taught my schoolchildren for so many years.

For the loving help they gave me, I thank Jean Mackenroth, Gerry Nelson, Ellen Allen, and Grace Geiger — all dear friends.

Thanks to Terry Burton, my photographer, who was so kind to come and work for me on a beautiful day in May.

I am grateful to my husband Ralph, my son Jim, and my daughter-in-law Joan for their trust in me and for providing me with a library of beautiful books.

I sincerely appreciate all the efforts of the editorial staff at Yankee Publishing Incorporated. I thank especially Clarissa Silitch, who encouraged me in the initial stages of this project, and Sharon Smith, who made my 1986 New Year's the best ever. To Cathryn Baskin, my editor, I extend a special thank you for her dedicated support and guidance.

Preface

As a young girl in elementary school in Detroit, I was fascinated by my art teacher's explanation of stencil work. She taught me that a stencil was just a fancy hole cut from a piece of paper. Stenciling challenged my imagination — though the process was simple, the possible repetitions and variations of images were endless.

Throughout my training and experience as an art teacher, my enthusiasm for this art form and method of reproducing designs remained with me. As my art teacher had done, I instructed schoolchildren that a stencil was just a fancy hole, which simplified this new undertaking for them and made possible many successful works of art. Their creative response was always new and exciting, no matter if the project was a stenciled handkerchief for Mother's Day, a large mural of prehistoric dinosaurs, or posters for a sock hop.

My love for beautiful quilts has been the foundation for my latest use of stencils. Early American appliquéd quilts inspired me to draft my own interpretations of traditional designs, and motifs from nature influenced designs for many more of my quilts. What a delight it has been for me to pursue this form of artistic expression! A quilt is a work of pleasure — a joy to make and a joy to own. It is my sincere wish to share with readers the satisfaction I've experienced in making this collection of stenciled quilts. ♡

7

PINEAPPLE URNS WITH OPEN ROSE BORDER,
67″ x 84″, whole-cloth stenciled quilt, circa 1820, Michigan.
Owner: Doris Reynolds Robinson, Traverse City, Michigan.

A Whole-Cloth Stenciled Quilt, circa 1820

This most magnificent example of a hand-stenciled quilt dates back to the 1820s. It is truly a museum piece and an especially cherished possession since there are so few Early American stenciled quilts remaining today.

When a Victorian dresser was purchased by an antique dealer in 1930 at a farm auction in central Michigan, this quilt was discovered tucked away in a lower drawer. What a find it was! Most known examples of early stenciled quilts have come from remote country areas, and this one was most likely made in Michigan by a rural farmer's wife.

Until the present owner finished hemming the edges in 1945, the quilt was never used, which is the reason for its splendid condition. The quiltmaker, however, did complete the stenciling, as well as the outline quilting of the stenciled components and the diamond, waffle-like quilting of the background. The quilting is an exceptional feature because many early stenciled quilts were not quilted, nor were they intended to be.

The whole-cloth quilt top, made of fine muslin, is actually composed of two large pieces of different widths that are sewn together with the smallest of stitches. One selvage edge shows in the seam joining the two pieces. The quilt top has a slight sheen, probably because the fabric has never been washed.

The quilt backing is made from recycled, coarsely woven fabric. The brownish stains were present in the fabric before it was incorporated into the quilt, and one section has a sewn-in patch. Tiny dark brown spots on the backing could be bloodstains from fingers that were pricked during the quilting process. The batting is a very thin layer of soft cotton.

The artist who did the stencil work on this quilt was very likely familiar with the work of other quilt stencilers of this period. The shading technique used for stenciling the open rose design is typical of quilts from New York and Connecticut, as are the little birds tucked in among the flowers. The stenciled rose leaves

detail, open rose border

9

in the border motif could have been traced from real rose leaves.

The artist obviously had a strong sense of good design. This quilt is an example of a very ambitious project, yet the many stenciled components are assembled into a harmonious whole. In the middle of the quilt, four urns containing floral patterns feature a pineapple as the central medallion. The bases of the urns form a prominent diamond, which is the focal point of the quilt. The delightful circle of grapes, rounded fruit, and flowers adds a rhythmic feeling around the urns, while the border of open roses with leaves forms a more solid pattern that helps to stabilize the overall design.

Each stenciled part is superbly executed with attention to the smallest detail. The painting is sharp and neatly done, and a close look reveals that many different stencils were used. The flowers and leaves are placed in slightly different positions in each of the urns, which indicates that each group was designed individually.

The main colors of the quilt are brick red, often fading to a light rose, and deep green, always painted solidly with no attempt at shading. The accent color used for the grapes is a dark blue, perhaps originally a Prussian blue, while ochre was used for the pineapple and some of the rounded fruit. Many of the connecting stems were painted with freehand brushstrokes. It is evident that the stenciling was done with oil-based paints. Brown marks surround many of the green stencils, indicating that the oil from the paint separated from the pigment and seeped into the fabric.

Certainly, this stenciled quilt is a jewel. It reflects the careful workmanship of an individual whose talents remain a part of our American heritage and, years later, inspire us to pursue this craft. ♡

detail, center urns with pineapples and floral patterns

Introduction

The itinerant artists of the 1800s — wall stencilers of New England — traveled the countryside with kits of dry paint, brushes, and an abundant supply of cut stencils. These artists displayed a wide range of skill and talent, but all used similar stenciling techniques. Often they mixed the dry paints with skimmed milk to ensure the permanence of the design. They applied the paint through stencils with a round, stiff-bristled brush or a dabber made from homespun fabric gathered onto the end of a padded stick.

The business of wall stenciling in New England communities was a good one. People no longer lived in crude log cabins and were now thinking of new, inexpensive ways to embellish their more elaborately constructed homes. Stenciling was the answer to many of their decorating problems, and they used the technique on walls, floors, and furnishings.

The stenciled pictures of the early 1800s, which were often painted on velvet and known as "theorem" paintings, marked the beginning of the fashion of fabric stenciling. The art of theorem painting had come originally from England, and its most common subjects were still-life arrangements and landscapes. Theorem landscapes, which were often enhanced by the addition of freehand painting, were more prevalent than the more rigid, primitive still-life designs. In many ways the theorem style and method of stenciling was a stepping-stone for the stenciled quilt.

It was during the first quarter of the nineteenth century that the use of stencils in quiltmaking came into existence. Just as wall stenciling was an imitation of expensive imported English wallpapers, so the early stenciled quilt was an imitation of the time-consuming appliqué of costly chintz, some of which was imported from India. Expensive English textiles of the 1800s inspired many of the complex floral stencil designs used for quilts. Flowers, fruit, and birds, which were common motifs in theorem still-life paintings, were also evident in early stenciled quilts.

The stenciled quilt and stenciled bedspread quickly became fashionable substitutes for delicately embroidered and appliquéd quilts. Unquilted stenciled spreads, which lacked an interlining and thus added little warmth, were used as bed covers in the summer months. Many of the quilted stenciled spreads or quilts that had interlinings were used for decorative display as well as for winter warmth.

The women who made these early stenciled quilts were quick to master the techniques. Stenciling was a craft, a creative decorative art that many could do and

enjoy. Most quiltmakers cut stencils from heavy oiled paper. They probably also used stencils cut from stiff leather and thin metal, materials that were used for wall and furniture stenciling. As in the technique for painting walls, quiltmakers painted the early quilt tops with a different stencil for each component and color. Each leaf and flower had its own stencil, and these were assembled at will to fashion and complete the planned design. At a later date, the artists adapted the use of single stencil patterns composed of many different parts of one design, which gave a more mass-produced appearance when painted.

The first stenciled quilt tops were made of whole cloth. When stenciling a whole-cloth quilt top, the artist probably started painting in the center and worked the design out toward the edge of the cloth. If the quilt was to have a pieced or patchwork top, the stenciled design could have been painted before the patches were pieced together with other patterned fabric, or the stenciling could have been done after the entire quilt top was assembled. Either way was acceptable, and the preferred method was dictated by the demands of the design.

For a period of about ten years — from 1824 to 1834 — the stenciled quilt was quite popular. The homemaker of this period was busy with the unending tasks of mothering, cooking, washing, mending, spinning, and weaving. The days were short and time was at a premium, and stenciling was an expedient way to add colorful, decorative touches to a home. Often simple objects and designs caught the homemaker's fancy and inspired her to copy the design. One early-1800s quiltmaker, for example, borrowed a horse pattern that was used in New England as a wall stencil and appeared even earlier on a 1724 Pennsylvania bed rug (a bed cover much like a hooked rug).

It also became a common and accepted practice to copy artwork from talented professional artists. This enabled the amateur artist to create works that otherwise were beyond his or her talents. Stencil patterns of Moses Eaton, Jr., (1796–1886), the noted wall stenciler of the towns of Hancock and Dublin, New Hampshire, have been found in homes well outside the area in which he worked. His handiwork was very popular and much in demand. To copy from Eaton or any professional artist gave distinction to the efforts of the novice.

Although stenciled quilts, bedspreads, tablecloths, table scarves, pillows, and curtains were common items in the 1800s, very few examples exist today because the poor-quality paint did not last. Setting these early colors was very difficult. Sometimes dye for yarn was used and mixed with gum arabic to create a good consistency for stencil painting, but the gum arabic added nothing to make the colors more permanent. Sometimes ground pigment would be mixed with oil and a mordant to make the colors fast. Often, however, these paints destroyed the fabric or faded away with wear and laundering.

The fabric that these early quiltmakers stenciled was usually spun and woven at home, often by the quiltmakers themselves or perhaps by other family members. Until the mid-1800s linen was more easily obtained than cotton, because flax was a common product of the early settlers' farms. Wide cloth was woven on looms and then sewn together to make a whole-cloth quilt top or backing for pieced-top quilts. Originally, plain white linen or cotton fabrics were used for backing, but not long after 1840, printed cotton fabric, known as calico, became a favored backing material.

Some early quiltmakers used wool batting as an interlining for their quilts. A wool interlining, though, with its traces of oily lanolin, often left brown stains on the quilt top after a period of years. Wool batting was more commonly used for comforters pieced from recycled, dark-colored clothing and tied off rather than quilted. These utilitarian quilts were used in the coldest weather because the wool gave a maximum of warmth.

The invention of the cotton gin in 1793 brought a new method of refining raw cotton in which all seeds were removed from the cotton fibers. This process produced a lightweight batting that could be used for quiltmaking and could be stitched easily with intricate quilting patterns. By the mid-1800s cotton batting was much preferred over wool batting for fancy pieced and appliquéd quilts.

In the mid-1800s the magnificent art of quiltmaking by hand was given a jolt by the appearance of the sewing machine. By 1846 it had become a prized possession in homes throughout America. Women became very inventive and quickly discovered that a quilt top could be pieced on a machine in a matter of days. Some women even used contrasting colored thread and quilted their quilts by machine, giving them a factory-made look.

From the outset, though, machine quilting was only a supplement to traditional hand quilting. After its initial introduction, machine quilting lost its popularity with quiltmakers, who found that nothing could take the place of hand quilting to embellish the intricate piecing of a patchwork or stenciled quilt. Many are still convinced today that the only way to make a fine quilt is to sew it entirely by hand. Needlework experts even believe that the back of a quilt should look as neatly sewn as the top, and this idea has merit, for it enables the quilt to be reversed for a new or different look.

Today, in our fast-moving society, it has become an accepted technique to use a sewing machine for piecing quilt tops if the machine stitches are concealed in a seam. When incorporated into a machine-sewn quilt, hand quilting can still give the appearance of a "best" quilt. The use of complex quilting designs such as plumes, spirals, wreaths, swags, and stars can put most machine-sewn quilts in the blue-ribbon class. The plus side for sewing patchwork designs by machine is that the quilt will be stronger and longer wearing and will take much less time to assemble.

The Early American stenciled quilt will always remain an integral part of our country's folk art. It is rather sad to remember that after 1835 the stenciled quilt lost its popularity, though it did regain some favor ten years later. By the end of 1860, however, the stenciled quilt had all but disappeared.

Splendid examples of stenciled spreads and quilts can be seen in museums across the country. To mention just a few: the Winterthur Museum in Winterthur, Delaware; the Shelburne Museum in Shelburne, Vermont; the Rockefeller Folk Art Center in Williamsburg, Virginia; and the Henry Ford Museum in Dearborn, Michigan. The American Museum in Bath, England, also houses a beautiful stenciled spread.

The present upsurge of interest in quiltmaking has generated quilts with distinctive and extraordinary characteristics. I hope contemporary quiltmakers will embrace again the art of stenciling quilts. No doubt, today's quiltmakers will bring a freshness to the quaint, primitive designs of the old stencil patterns, which are a unique and priceless heritage of the early makers of stenciled quilts.   ♡

"Art is a compulsion to share an enriched vision with others."

— *James J. McBride*

PART ONE

The Quilts

When a quilt is designed around a stencil pattern, the stencil becomes the life of the quilt. Color knows no bounds, and the design need not be confined to just one pattern. The limitless, often spontaneous combination of colors and patterns lends an excitement to stenciled quilts and offers a creative potential found in no other form of quiltmaking.

The stenciled quilts shown on the following pages are distinctly contemporary, even though some have motifs taken from Early American appliquéd quilts. Most stenciled quilts, in fact, closely resemble appliquéd quilts, since the outline quilting of the stenciled designs is similar to the relief of hand-stitched appliqué. The beauty of stenciled quilts is that they eliminate the tedious process but retain the delicate and striking feeling of appliqué.

All the quilts in this collection were hand painted from original stencil patterns created by the author and were completely hand quilted and hand finished. Most are quilted with outline stitching worked around the stenciled designs. Some are also quilted along the seams. One has a quilted, stenciled design that nearly covers the entire quilt top. A couple, which should be classified as comforters, have no quilting at all but are

tied off with strands of colored wool yarns. Several others use this tying technique to accent the hand quilting and overall design.

Several of the quilts are constructed with whole-cloth quilt tops made from a single piece of fabric, often a bed sheet. Some of these whole-cloth quilts have quilting lines that simulate pieced squares, and some are enhanced with machine-appliquéd fabric strips.

Most of the quilts are constructed with patchwork, or pieced, tops, in which blocks and other pieces of fabric are sewn together by machine to make the large quilt top. The blocks are usually pieced together in a specific pattern to form a row, and the rows are repeated or alternated to make the overall pattern of the quilt top. These stenciled patchwork quilts are composed of simply pieced patterns so that the stencil design remains the focal point.

There has been no attempt with any of the quilts to simulate the characteristics of an old heirloom. The polyester/cotton–blend fabrics are crease resistant. The bonded polyester-fiber batting used for the interlining is lightweight and warm, dries quickly, and does not mat easily when laundered. The hand quilting needed for joining the quilt top, interlining, and backing is kept to a minimum. There's no need to secure these modern

materials with rows of quilting stitches an inch apart, as was thought to have been necessary in years past.

Indeed, the plump batting used today billows up with only intermittent lines of quilting stitches. This often gives the quilt the look of *trapunto*, a traditional method of quilting in which a design is outline quilted and extra padding is inserted from the back side of the quilt. The high relief of the padded design creates an elegant three-dimensional effect on the quilt's surface.

Are stenciled quilts quicker to make than conventional quilts? The answer depends on how the quilt top is constructed. If the quilt top is made of whole cloth, it demands a carefully planned stencil layout but often can be assembled relatively quickly and easily. If, on the other hand, the quilt top is pieced with complicated patterns to be stenciled, the quilt can be quite challenging and will take a longer time to assemble.

The Rose Wreath and Bud quilt (cover and color plate 25) was my very first effort in creating a stenciled quilt. I was feeling my way, starting small and gathering courage as I went along. I remember how excited I was as I quilted around the stenciled parts of the design and watched them puff up like trapunto work.

Perhaps the most enjoyable quilt I made in this collection was the Art Deco quilt (color plate 28). I've always welcomed the challenge of large-scale drawing and felt free and uninhibited when creating the large, flowing contours for the cattails and dragonflies. Moreover, the whole-cloth top released me from the time-consuming preparation of the quilt top.

Planning the Art Nouveau quilt (color plate 21) occupied more time than planning any of the other quilts and far exceeded the time required for cutting and painting the stencils. Drawing the large stencil of the girl's head was complex; laying out and marking precisely the large oval and the outer borders took patience; and marking the ties an inch apart on the background was tedious. Yet once I began quilting the girl's head and could see how unusual the quilt was going to be, hours of work went by quickly. And the finished quilt has given me great satisfaction.

If you've ever done stenciling of any kind or have seen stenciling demonstrated, you'll have little difficulty making your first stenciled quilt. And if you're already an accomplished quiltmaker, you'll appreciate adding these stenciling techniques to your repertoire. No matter what your level of skill or artistic talent, the variety of stenciled quilts and specific instructions provided in this book will help you create a quilt you can cherish.

Stencil designs are appealing and versatile. They can be conservative or bold, but they're always commanding. If your home reflects the country look or has Early American accents, there are many quilts you can make exactly as shown or adapt to harmonize with your furnishings. If your home is decorated in a contemporary style, a stenciled quilt done in an art deco style could easily become the focal point of any room.

But no matter what style you choose, by creating a stenciled quilt you'll enrich your home with a future heirloom and enjoy many hours pursuing this unique combination of two traditional American crafts. And perhaps most significant, by applying present-day artistic techniques and ideas, you'll be contributing to the evolution of this unique approach to quiltmaking. ♡

color plate 1, opposite page:
WILD ROSE, 39″ x 53″, patchwork quilt with stenciled blocks.

This quilt is a variation of a pinwheel leaf design and traditional wild rose design. The combination of leaves and blossoms creates a dainty pattern, and the outline quilting of the flowers gives the effect of trapunto work. Note also the wall stenciling around the window casing (see the instructions in Part Four).

color plate 2, right:
SWEETHEART, 69″ x 86″, whole-cloth quilt with appliqué and stenciled design.

This whole-cloth quilt has machine-appliquéd strips and hearts. The outline quilting of the stenciled lovebirds sets them off as an important part of the quilt design, and a border of small stenciled hearts balances the rest of the quilt. The bows add a feminine flair. Notice that the background is quilted with a heart design, which emphasizes the theme.

color plate 3, left:
SCOTCH THISTLE, 56″ x 78″, patchwork quilt with stenciled blocks.

The Scotch Thistle stencil creates a contemporary-looking quilt that also has the look of *scherenschnitte* (Pennsylvania Dutch scissors-cutting) because of the silhouetted symmetry of the stencil design. The stenciled blocks, which are set in a diamond pattern, contrast with the blocks made from a small gray calico print. The thistle blocks are quilted a half-inch from the seams, and the quilting design of the other blocks is large and simple.

color plate 4, left:
AMERICAN TULIP, 47″ x 68″, patchwork quilt with stenciled blocks.

The legend-filled tulip design was a favorite of the Pennsylvania Dutch. The flower was easy to draw and made a pleasant pattern, typical of country motifs. The six large stenciled squares in this quilt are set into a diamond pattern, and the bright red sash strips act as a picture frame. The quilting on the calico squares echoes the stencil design.

color plate 5, above:
CHRISTMAS STAR, 67″ x 95″, whole-cloth quilt with appliqué and stenciled design.

This contemporary quilt depicts the five-pointed Christmas star. Each star is created by the striped fabric that surrounds it, which is pieced and appliquéd. Ten green stenciled pine trees encircle each star to complete the design. The trees and stars are outline quilted and tied with red yarn.

color plate 6, left:
COUNTRY CHICKENS, 65″ x 85″, patchwork quilt with stenciled blocks.

Chickens capture the country look, and perhaps this quilt would be at home as a wall hanging in a kitchen. The blocks are quilted along the seams, and the calico print is accented with ties of black yarn. This patchwork pattern is sometimes called Rail Fence. The stenciled floor also adds to the country look (see the instructions in Part Four).

color plate 7, opposite page:
BIRDS OF A FEATHER, 41″ x 55″, patchwork quilt
with stenciled blocks.

This quilt was inspired by a greeting card from the
Smithsonian Institution that showed an appliquéd quilt
made about 1850 in New York State. Notice the
texture on the tree trunks, which was produced by
stencil painting through a piece of window screen. The
design is fully outline quilted.

color plate 8, right:
WHIG ROSE (sometimes known as Democrat Rose),
45″ x 59″, patchwork quilt with stenciled blocks.

A quilt made in Indiana in 1855 furnished the idea for
this quilt. The rose-colored fabric was chosen to
harmonize with the rose design, and the flower stencils
are outline quilted. The canvas floorcloth is stenciled
with the same design (see the instructions in Part Four).

color plate 9, left:
TEDDY BEAR, 40″ x 50″, whole-cloth
quilt with stenciled design.

Three different colors were used to stencil
these teddy bears, which are laid out in a
hit-and-miss plan. The selection of a dotted
fabric made the diagonal background
quilting a breeze. Each bear is fully outline
quilted and has accent lines drawn with a
black felt-tip laundry marker. This stencil
pattern is just right for a baby's bib too (see
the instructions in Part Four).

color plate 10, right:

HOLLY WREATH, 48″ x 67″, patchwork quilt with stenciled blocks.

Small, delicate green holly leaves and red berries form circles to create this bright Christmas quilt. The window-pane strips carry the red color throughout the design. The quilt is quilted along the seams and tied off with dark green yarn. Notice the stenciled canvas log carrier in the background (see the instructions in Part Four).

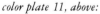

color plate 11, above:

RUNNING RABBITS, 31″ x 50″, whole-cloth quilt with stenciled design.

These three baby quilts show how just a change in color can alter the appearance of a design. Use these as an example when planning a quilt. Experiment with many colors — the results can be surprising. A simple whole-cloth quilt of this size makes a good project for a beginner.

color plate 12, right:

LEAF AND CHAIN, 52″ x 72″, patchwork quilt with stenciled strips.

Width-wise strips make this contemporary quilt look wider than it is. The design is clean and bold. The quilting reflects the same design as the stencil and is simple and uncluttered. A variation of the stencil pattern was used for the hand-stenciled, hand-quilted fabric on the chair. Notice too the stenciling on the fireplace screen. (For both of these smaller projects, see the instructions in Part Four).

color plate 13, below:
VICTORIAN CRAZY QUILT, 45″ x 67″, patchwork quilt with embroidery and stenciled blocks.

Crazy quilts were popular from 1880 to 1890, and almost all of them were made from elegant fabrics like silk, satin, and velvet. This crazy quilt is a parlor throw, embellished by a great variety of embroidery stitches. It is also endowed with stenciled long-stemmed American Beauty roses. One thickness of muslin was used in place of polyester-fiber batting. Each block is quilted along the seams.

color plate 14, above:
ROSE WREATH WITH TULIPS, 35½″ x 51″, patchwork quilt with stenciled blocks.

The Rose Wreath pattern of this quilt dates to 1840 and has many variations. The bright blue and green colors used here are reminiscent of early Pennsylvania Dutch quilts. This quilt was made as a wall hanging but could also be used as a table runner.

color plate 15, right:
TURKEY TRACKS, 60″ x 78″, whole-cloth quilt
with stenciled design.

Wandering Foot was another name often given to this
quilt pattern. The straight quilting lines define the
design, giving this whole-cloth quilt the appearance of a
pieced quilt. Each part of the stenciled design is outline
quilted.

color plate 16, below right:
SONG BIRDS, 33″ x 47″, patchwork quilt with
stenciled blocks.

This small quilt was made expressly for use as a wall
hanging. The outline quilting of the stencils gives
dimension to the design, and the quilting on the tan
strips strengthens the overall plan of the quilt. The blue
stenciled table cover adds a decorative, protective touch
(see the instructions in Part Four).

color plate 17, below:
ROSE OF SHARON (sometimes called the
Whig Rose), 39½″ x 53″, patchwork quilt with
stenciled blocks.

Each quiltmaker of the 1800s personalized this rose
design, and their alterations have caused much
confusion among the rose patterns and names. The
separate cluster of petals in the center of the design
makes this pattern more elaborate than most rose
designs. Each stenciled part is outline quilted. The soft
blue and green colors add much to this quilt.

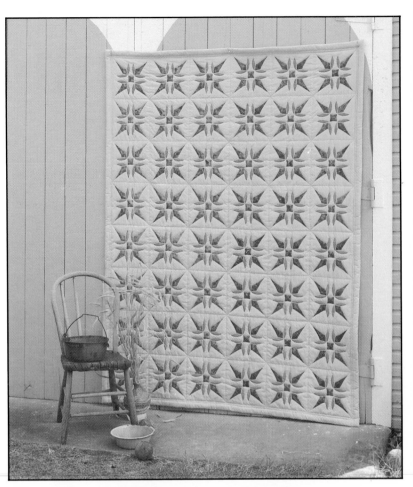

color plate 18, left:
CIRCLE OF TULIPS, 47″ x 61″, patchwork quilt with stenciled blocks.

Green leaves swirl around to carry the attention from one tulip to another, while the hearts in the center of the design help to stabilize the motion. The border reflects the same delicate feeling as the tulip design, and the quilting on the mullion strips enhances the composition.

color plate 19, above:
HEARTS AND FLOWERS, 57″ x 66″, patchwork quilt with stenciled blocks.

The sharp contrast of black stenciled hearts and tulips on muslin and green calico print gives a feeling of an early Amish quilt. Every part of the stencil pattern is outline quilted, creating a strong texture. The solid black border contains the bold quilt design.

color plate 20, left:
CREEPING PERIWINKLE, 67″ x 72″, patchwork quilt with stenciled strips.

This quilt is composed of long, pieced strips of fabric. The stencil design echoes the tiny flowers of the striped calico print. Circle quilting around each stenciled flower accentuates the design even further. The vertical strips are quilted along the seams, adding an illusion of length to the quilt.

color plate 21, right:

ART NOUVEAU, 63″ x 76″, whole-cloth quilt with stenciled design.

For a brief twenty years (1890–1910), the art nouveau movement was popular. It featured themes from nature and human figures that were stylized with a French influence. The girl on this quilt is typical of the era. The outline quilting of the stenciled design is accented with ties that create a textured background. The large center design was cut from brown kraft paper that withstood one stencil painting very well.

color plate 22, left:

BLUE WHIG ROSE, 68½″ x 83″, patchwork quilt with stenciled blocks.

This quilt was inspired by an appliqué quilt made in 1861. The exacting stenciled squares are outlined with a small stencil pattern that accentuates the main design. The quilting on the mullion strips pulls the overall design together. The color scheme was kept very simple.

color plate 23, above left:
DUTCH TULIPS, 53½″ x 74½″,
patchwork quilt with stenciled blocks.

Here the Pennsylvania tulip takes on a more modern look. The six large tulip squares are set together with a simple nine-patch pattern and are quilted along the seams. The tulips are outline quilted. The light patches in the nine-patch blocks are quilted with a circle, and all patches are tied in the center with a harmonizing aqua yarn.

color plate 24, above right:
HEARTS AND MORE HEARTS, 47″ x 65″, patchwork quilt with stenciled blocks.

Because this quilt lacks hand quilting, it should be classified as a comforter. It is made of pieced nine-patch blocks that alternate with larger stenciled blocks. In the nine-patch blocks, the stenciled hearts appear only on the plain muslin patches, creating a subtle contrast with the small calico print of the other patches. The comforter has an extra-thick batting and is tied off with muslin-colored yarn so as not to detract from the stenciled design.

color plate 25, left:
ROSE WREATH AND BUD, 38½″ x 52″, patchwork quilt with stenciled blocks.

When the buds were added, this old pattern of the 1850s took on a delicate touch. The quilting stitches are held close to the stenciled design, which gives an illusion of trapunto work without the traditional stuffing. The quilt is the size of a throw and could also be used as a wall hanging.

color plate 26, below:
CHRISTMAS ROSE OF SHARON, 43″ x 57″, patchwork
quilt with stenciled blocks.

The bright red and green color scheme of this quilt makes it a
nice Christmas accent, and the outline quilting of the stencil
patterns gives it an old-fashioned look. Used under the Christmas
tree, the quilt takes on a new function. Small quilts like this one
can be made within a week.

color plate 27, right:
OAK LEAF AND REEL, 44″ x 58″, patchwork quilt
with stenciled blocks.

A New England appliqué pattern of 1840, the Oak Leaf design
is one that signifies longevity. In old quilts, oak leaves were often
combined with flower and squash motifs. This quilt uses a reel to
balance the oak leaf motif. The stenciled canvas floorcloth has the
same Oak Leaf and Reel design as the quilt (see the instructions
in Part Four). A simple change in color gives a different effect.

color plate 28, opposite page:
ART DECO, 62″x 78½″, whole-cloth quilt with stenciled design.

Art deco flourished during the 1920s and was influenced by the
art nouveau era that preceded it. The simplifying of dragonflies
and cattails gives this quilt its modern look. The dark blue sheet
used for the quilt top creates a subtle background that
complements the painted stencils, making them look fresh and
glamorous. The extra-large stencils were cut from lightweight
cardboard suit boxes. The design is completely outline quilted.

color plate 29, right:
LAUREL LEAF, 45″ x 59″, patchwork quilt with stenciled blocks.

The design of this quilt was influenced by an 1865 quilt that displayed a classic design brought to America during the Napoleonic era. The outline quilting sets the leaves in relief and gives a pleasant dimension to the quilt.

color plate 30, below:
PETER RABBIT, 52″ x 61″, patchwork quilt with stenciled blocks.

Every child should have his or her own Peter Rabbit quilt. This one is pieced, with plain blocks setting off the stenciled blocks. The fabric is soft outing flannel, which makes the quilt ever so cuddly and warm. All blocks are quilted along the seams, and the plaid blocks are tied off with matching tan yarn. The stenciled rabbits are accentuated by lines made with a black felt-tip laundry marker. The pillow in the crib was made with scraps that were left over from the quilt top (see the instructions in Part Four).

color plate 31, right:
WHIRL OF MAPLE LEAVES, 52″ x 69″, patchwork quilt with stenciled blocks.

These stenciled maple leaves reflect the many bright colors of the fall. The blended paints add variety and movement to the whirling leaves. This patchwork quilt is not quilted but is tied off with red and green yarn in the traditional style of a comforter.

color plate 32, below:
TRUE OAK LEAVES, 56″ x 84″, patchwork quilt with stenciled blocks.

For the more timid would-be artist, there is always an easy way out — nature! The oak leaves used to make these stencil patterns were real. The quilting on this pieced quilt was kept simple, accenting the circles of the design.

color plate 33, right:
PINEAPPLE, 60½″ x 73″, patchwork quilt with stenciled blocks.

The ever-popular pineapple was a colonial symbol of hospitality. This pieced quilt is made in the old heirloom tumbler pattern and set together with calico strips. The color of the stenciled pineapples harmonizes with the calico strips. The upright blocks of stenciled pineapples are outline quilted, and the plain inverted blocks are quilted from the same stencil pattern. Each block is also quilted along the seams.

color plate 34, opposite page:
THEOREM THEME, 62½″ x 89½″, whole-cloth quilt with appliqué and stenciled design.

The theorem-style stencil painting in the center is the subject and focal point of this quilt. Machine-appliquéd striped fabric frames the painting. The striped fabric is quilted along the seams, and diamond quilting fills the background. The theorem still-life painting on the easel was painted from the same stencils used on the quilt. Note that the stencil design on the canvas tote bag is the same as the one used on the quilt borders (see the instructions in Part Four). The grapes were omitted on the quilt to simplify the design.

"Art is the demonstration that the ordinary is extraordinary."

— *Amedee Ozenfant*

PART TWO

The Stencil

Stenciling on fabric can produce better results than painting on other surfaces, and the techniques are simple and easy to master. The only worrisome thing is to avoid making mistakes, since paint is not easily removed from unwanted spots. But if you stay alert and develop a slow, methodical approach to your work, your efforts will be rewarded.

All the stencil patterns in this book are composed of a fancy hole or series of holes that are cut from the stencil material. The area separating two or more holes is called a *bridge* and should never be cut away. The bridges strengthen the stencil material and form an important part of the pattern by adding interest to the design. There is no rule as to how wide the bridges should be — the design itself makes the demands.

Making the Stencil

Materials. There are many different types of stencil materials from which to choose. A few of the most common materials are Mylar and other brands of tough, frosted or clear plastic; semitransparent, waxed stenciling paper; and heavy yellow cardboard. Two-ply Bristol board or tagboard also makes a sturdy stencil.

Mylar stencils are durable and last a long time, but Mylar can be more difficult to cut than the other materials. Although it comes in a variety of thicknesses, what you'll want is 3mm to 5mm Mylar (you might also find it under "drafting films" at a local drafting supplier). Stencils made from frosted Mylar are easier to use than those made from clear Mylar. Mylar is inexpensive, often sold in packages of 10 or 12 sheets (about 12″ x 18″), or as single sheets (about 24″ x 36″). Some art stores will cut sheets of Mylar to your specifications.

Because of the popularity of Mylar and other plastic stencil materials, some arts and crafts stores no longer stock waxed stencil paper. If you do use waxed stencil paper and if the quilt is large and requires a lot of painting, it is best to cut three or four stencils at the start, since the patterns will wear out. Just tape all the thicknesses of stencil paper together when cutting so the pieces will not move.

For very large stencil patterns, you can improvise by using lightweight cardboard boxes. Although the instructions in Part Three recommend Mylar, you may want to experiment with several types of stencil materials to find the one best suited to your work habits.

Tracing or Copying. When you've chosen a stencil pattern, center it on the stencil material and leave an extra-wide border around the pattern. Leave a 1″ border if

you'll be painting with small stencil brushes and a 1½" to 2" border if you'll be using larger 1" brushes. The borders will prevent the paint-filled brush from smudging the fabric while you're stenciling.

Mark the pattern carefully on the stencil material with a black fine-tip felt pen. Semitransparent materials such as Mylar can be placed with the frosted side up directly over the original pattern, which can then be traced. If you use opaque stencil materials like cardboard, the pattern should be copied with carbon paper. Place the carbon side of the paper face down on the top side of the cardboard, and slip both pieces under the pattern to be copied. Then trace the outline of the stencil pattern.

Most of the stencil patterns in this book are full size and have been reproduced directly from the author's original designs. Although some of the patterns were too large to fit on a page, it's easy to reproduce them. Each of these patterns is symmetrical, so trace one side of the pattern first, then turn the stencil material and trace the corresponding side to complete the design. (The stencil patterns can also be adapted for use as quilting templates.)

The small patterns printed on grids for a couple of the quilts must be transferred onto paper with larger grids before they can be used for making stencils. The grids have a scale of 1 square = 1 inch. Count the number of grid squares on the small pattern, and draw corresponding 1" grid squares on a large piece of paper. Then, starting at the outer edge of the small pattern, count the number of squares to the point where the drawing begins. Find the corresponding square on the large paper, and draw only the part of the design shown in that square. Continue drawing the pattern square by square. When the enlarged drawing is finished, trace it onto the stencil material.

Cutting. The secret of a good stencil lies in how well it has been cut. Any of the stencil materials mentioned above can be cut with a single-edge razor blade, a utility knife, or a No. 1 graphic arts knife (manufactured by X-acto and other companies) with a No. 11 blade. Always cut with a new sharp blade. Electric stencil-cutting pens are also available for cutting plastic stencil materials like Mylar. These pens cut with heat so only light pressure is needed, and several stencils can be cut at one time.

To cut the stencil, place the stencil material on a sheet of ¼"-thick glass (cover the edges of the glass with masking tape). Hold the cutting knife as you would a pencil. Pierce the stencil material with the point of the knife on the cutting line of the design. Do not move the hand holding the knife, but with your free hand, palm down, gently feed the stencil material into the knife. If you have problems using the knife, you can cut the Mylar with sharp, pointed embroidery scissors.

Smaller parts of the design should be cut before the larger parts to maintain the structural strength of the stencil material for as long as possible. Mistakes can be patched by applying transparent or masking tape to both sides of the stencil material. Keep the cut stencils flat, and never fold the stencil materials.

With some stencil patterns, you'll need two or more separate stencils for painting parts of the pattern in different colors. Take a few precautions when making each stencil to make sure that the parts of the design will be faithfully superimposed on top of each other when you paint. Square up the edges of each sheet to keep the design in the correct position. Make a registration mark, such as "top," in the same place on each sheet so that each part of the design will line up correctly.

Preparing to Paint

Paints. A variety of paints suitable for stenciling are available in art stores and from mail-order businesses (see the list of suppliers on page 158); some of these paints are made specifically for applying on fabric. When selecting paint for a stenciled quilt, consider also the acrylic paints available in art supply stores and recommended in the instructions in Part Three. Most artist-brand acrylic paints come in tubes and have a toothpaste-like consistency that's just right for stencil painting. An added advantage is that these paints can be cleaned up easily with soap and warm water.

A solid oil-based paint in stick form also works well on fabric. A dry brush is used to distribute the paint, which is applied to the stencil material around the stencil opening and then worked into the fabric. These paints come in a kit, and a solvent or turpentine is used for cleanup.

Permanent acrylic fabric-painting dyes are available in squeeze bottles. These dyes can be mixed with an extender medium to slow the drying process. Cleanup is done with soap and water.

Don't rule out decorator interior or exterior latex house paints. Many exciting colors can be custom mixed, giving your quilt or other stenciled project an exceptional flair. These decorator house paints may be a bit thin and may leave a crusty surface on the fabric if applied too heavily. But with care in painting they can give very good results.

Brushes. An assortment of round, stiff-bristled stencil brushes ranging in size from No. 4 (⅜") to No. 8 (½") is nice to have. A 1" brush is good for very large stencils. Beginners should use a small brush, such as a No. 4, until they've mastered the techniques of handling the

Above: stippling over chicken wire

Below: stippling over hardware cloth

brush and controlling the paint. Because larger brushes hold more paint, they're usually harder to control.

Miscellaneous Supplies. The other materials necessary for stenciling can be found among ordinary household supplies. A large white ceramic plate or platter makes a good palette. If leftover paint is allowed to dry on the palette, it will create a rough-textured surface. In subsequent painting sessions, the paint-filled stencil brush can be worked over the dried paint to help distribute the paint evenly on the brush.

A large water jar is important, and terry cloth, such as an old bath towel, makes a good paint rag. Make sure all brushes are clean before you start, and if necessary, clean them with soap and warm water. For cleaning stubborn dried acrylic paint, use alcohol. It is always best to stencil with a dry brush, so vigorously rub the clean brushes on terry cloth to remove all moisture.

Painting on Fabric

Before painting, wash all fabric to remove sizing and to prevent further shrinking. Iron the damp fabric completely dry, removing all wrinkles. Trim away all selvage edges.

If the stenciled quilt top is to be made of whole cloth, plan the stencil layout on the fabric before you begin to paint. Stencil patterns can be centered on the fabric by using crease lines that are pressed with a warm iron. This type of guideline will help you avoid using pencil marks, which are very hard to remove.

If the quilt top is to be patchwork, the painting should take place after the entire quilt top is stitched so that the stencil pattern can be centered precisely on each block. Cutting the stencil material to fit just inside the block will make centering the stencil much easier. If necessary, you can tape extra pieces of paper to the edges of the stencil material so the paintbrush will not smudge the surrounding fabric. If a mishap should occur during the painting, the single quilt block can be replaced with a new one.

When you're ready to start painting, use masking tape to secure the stencil pattern to the patchwork block or whole-cloth fabric. A moving stencil is very frustrating and could easily contribute to a disaster.

Apply the paint to the brush very sparingly. Work the paint into the tip of the brush, making sure there are no extra blobs of paint. When in doubt, test the paint-filled brush on a fabric sample. If the acrylic paint is too thick, it can be thinned by adding a tad of water.

Apply the paint through the hole of the stencil with a gentle dabbing motion. Work from the outer edge of the stencil hole toward the center of the opening

Left: streaking, with accent lines added with a marking pen

to lessen the possibility of paint seeping under the stencil. The paint should be worked into the surface of the fabric, but not so much that it will soak through to the back side.

When using more than one color on a single stencil, paint just one color at a time and block out the other color sections with masking tape. This will help eliminate the danger of inadvertently applying paint where it was not intended. While you're painting, the back of the stencil material must be kept clean at all times. Do this often by putting the stencil bottom side up between two paper towels, placing it on a smooth, flat surface, and smoothing your hand over the towel on the bottom side of the stencil. The towels will absorb any paint that might have seeped under the stencil opening. Be sure to check frequently for excess paint.

Painting fabric with acrylic paints can be done quickly. If the paint is applied sparingly, it dries to the touch in a few seconds. This allows the stencil to be moved and reused near or over newly painted areas.

Unfortunately, there is no sure way to correct a painting error on fabric. If you do make a small mistake, try to remove the paint with a wet, warm, soapy cloth. This can be done successfully only if the paint is fresh and in an isolated area, separated from other stenciled parts. If this procedure cannot be followed, let the paint dry completely, and then scrape it lightly with a sharp razor blade. Take care not to fray the surface of the fabric. Alcohol can be used for lifting dried paint, but it may leave a dirty ring in the fabric.

All paint should cure-dry overnight, and then the colors must be set with a dry, hot iron. Moving the iron slowly, iron the back side and then the front side of the painted area. A pressing cloth will prevent scorching. If proper care is taken in setting, most acrylic paints will withstand many washings. Avoid using bleach compounds when laundering, however.

After stenciling, paint-filled brushes should be placed in water — dried acrylic paint is almost impossible to remove from paintbrushes. Mylar stencils can be reused and should be cleaned after each stenciling session. If you soak the stencil in warm water, the paint will lift and separate from the stencil with the aid of the paintbrush. Even old paint-covered stencils can be reclaimed with a little work.

If you are unsure about your ability to paint without making mistakes, you may want to choose a small quilt, tote bag, or another simple project so you can gain confidence and skill. The most important thing to remember is to stay alert. The painting techniques are simple, but you must stay one step ahead of yourself to anticipate the unexpected.

Stenciling Techniques

Keep in mind as you work that the stenciling on a quilt, be it of whole cloth or patchwork, sets your quilt apart from all others. Each stenciler brings a unique way of applying paint that makes his or her work as distinctly personal as one's handwriting. There are no set rules governing stencil work, so you always have free rein. And remember that each leaf, each flower, each part of a design can show its own personality. Nothing ever has to be painted the same way all the time.

Textures. Stencil painting need not have a solid appearance to be well done — in fact, half the enjoyment of stenciling is creating different textures. Do some creative thinking and seek out strange props, such as window screen or hardware mesh, to produce textures that appear interesting.

Many pleasing effects can be achieved by simply streaking the stencil brush over the fabric. When the paint-filled brush is streaked across an opening in the stencil of a leaf, the very movement of the brush will create a feeling of rhythm. Stippling, dabbing, or pouncing the paint-filled stencil brush will also give a variety of effects. Develop your own ways of producing different textures, and practice the techniques illustrated in the stencils shown throughout this section.

Colors. There are so many interesting things to learn about colors. Red, for instance, suggests courage and vitality; yellow typifies light, such as the sun; and blue means truth and wisdom. These three primary colors can be used to produce all other colors (see the color

Right: stippling over extruded metal

wheel on page 40). Mixing two primary colors produces one of the three secondary colors — orange, green, and violet. Mixing one primary color and one secondary color produces one of the six colors of the intermediate group. Black can be made by mixing the three primary colors, and brown can be made by mixing orange and blue.

Color has three physical properties: *hue, value,* and *intensity.* Hue is the artist's term for color, and value is related to the amount of light in a color. A color's value can range from very light, sometimes known as a *pastel,* to very dark, often called a *shade.*

Below: streaking and stippling over metal window screen

stippling

When you stencil paint, it is always wise to work the colors from light to dark to maintain complete control of the paint. A color can be concentrated to give a darker shade, but it is impossible to lift the paint once it has been applied. A lighter color can be achieved by adding white paint.

Intensity refers to the brightness or dullness of a color. Red at its greatest intensity is the most vibrant color, and red and green used next to each other in their strongest intensities will give the illusion of vibrating colors. Bright intense colors also produce afterimages of opposite colors on the color wheel. Saturating the eye

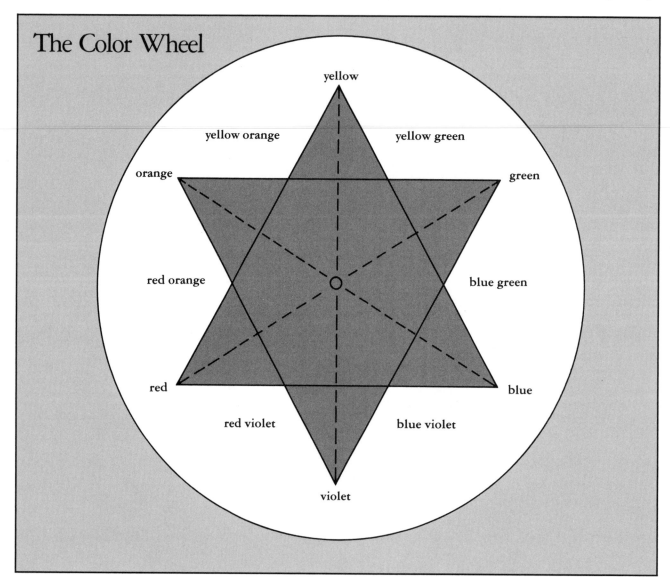

The Color Wheel

yellow

yellow orange   yellow green

orange   green

red orange   blue green

red   blue

red violet   blue violet

violet

with a very intense red will cause an afterimage of green, and so on.

Bright intense colors may not always be the answer for a color scheme, however. Any color can be toned down by adding a little of its complementary color, which lies directly opposite it on the color wheel. It is best to use a complementary color rather than black to tone down a color, because colors added to colors allow them to remain clear and vital and produce a richer tone. Once black is added, the colors often become muddy and unattractive.

Mixing colors is fun. Experiment!

Designing Original Patterns

Creating your own stencil patterns can bring a satisfaction that's hard to equal. The first thing you must do when designing a pattern is to analyze your needs. Where and how will the stencil be used? Should the design echo the print of a fabric or wallpaper, or a pattern in an accent rug? Should the colors contrast or harmonize with the existing colors? Should the scale of the stencil design be large or small?

If you decide to make a stencil from an existing printed design, simply trace the design and make allowances in the drawing for bridges. But developing an original design can be most satisfying of all. Plan your sketch with bridges. Suppose, for example, that you want to make a stencil for a simple sunflower that has a button-like center. If you draw the flower as usual and then cut around the outline, the center will drop out. To make the design work as a stencil, draw the flower with bridges separating the petals and center, making an individual hole for each part of the flower.

Keep in mind that narrow bridges create a delicate feeling, while wide bridges make the design bold. Gather your ideas and arrange them on paper. Trace a line with your pencil to explore a design. Work the idea and the line over and over again until it is saying what you want to hear. The design must make a forceful statement on the fabric. The color scheme should make it sing. Be inspired! ♡

shading with streaking

"If you get simple beauty and naught else, you get about the best thing God invents."

— *Robert Browning*

PART THREE

The Making of a Quilt

Before starting work on a quilt, read through its instructions and these general instructions completely. Check the required materials and supplies, the size, and the level of difficulty. If you want the quilt to fit a particular bed, measure the bed, taking the drop of the quilt on the sides of the bed into consideration. The quilt can be made large enough to fall to the floor, or it can be left shorter and used with a dust ruffle — a matter of personal taste.

Each quilt in this book is classified as beginning, intermediate, or advanced (for quick reference, see the table on page 49). These levels take into account the complexity of constructing the quilt top as well as the complexity of the stenciling procedures. The techniques required for painting very large stencil patterns put several quilts at the advanced level, even though the preparation of the quilt tops themselves may be relatively simple.

Make an honest appraisal of your sewing abilities and painting skills before you select any of these quilts for your first project. Starting with a small challenge will do wonders in building your self-confidence and lead to greater rewards later on. If your sewing skills are good, you'll have little or no problem constructing any of the patchwork quilt tops. And if you choose to make an advanced quilt, don't be intimidated — many times a difficult procedure can be mastered with a little forethought and discipline.

Planning and Preparing

Fabric. The selection of fabrics can make hand quilting a joy — *or* a work of extended labor. Muslin can be quilted with ease and is readily available in solid colors and prints. Muslin and calico come in widths ranging from 32″ to 45″, depending on the manufacturer. All fabrics selected for a quilt should be smooth in texture and of similar weight.

Many of the quilts use bed sheets for the top or backing. Choose sheets with a low thread count, from 120 to 150 threads per inch. Avoid using sheets with a high thread count (from 160 to 180 or more threads per inch), such as fine percale, since it is very difficult to sew through such tightly woven fabrics with a short quilting needle. Loosely woven fabrics that ravel easily and highly textured, stiff, or heavy fabrics should also be avoided in quiltmaking.

Batting. Nearly all the quilts in this book use bonded polyester-fiber batting as an interlining. This batting is made especially for quiltmaking and comes in different lofts or thicknesses, ranging from ¼″ to 3″. A low- or medium-loft batting works well for a stenciled quilt, but this can vary depending on how thick you wish your quilt to be.

Most manufacturers make batting to fit standard-size beds, including cribs. Batting sizes (in inches) vary but usually run as follows:

Crib	45 x 60
Twin	72 x 90
Full	81 x 96
Queen	90 x 108
King	120 x 120

Many arts and crafts stores stock large rolls of batting that can be cut by the yard. Plan to buy batting several inches larger than the actual size of the quilt. Sometimes the batting will shift during quilting, and it is best to make allowances for this.

Other Supplies. Have a sharp pair of scissors, a ruler or yardstick, and a good supply of straight and safety pins on hand. You'll also need a sharpened No. 3 (hard) lead pencil or dressmaker's marking pencil, a tape measure, and a seam ripper. For sewing a patchwork quilt top together, choose a cotton-covered polyester thread that matches the color of the top. A No. 50 thread will make a strong seam.

Make sure you have the supplies required for stenciling. You'll need about half a tube of acrylic paint if the stencil pattern and quilt are large. If the pattern and quilt are small, several teaspoons of paint will suffice. A few quilts call for additional supplies, such as a piece of window screen.

Making a Quilt Top

Cutting Fabric. The fabric must be accurately cut to the size specified for each quilt. Always cut away the selvage edge — it is tightly woven and will usually shrink when washed. For patchwork tops, cut the square or rectangular blocks along the straight grain of the fabric to make the quilt top stronger and sewing easier.

Before cutting the fabric, plan out and measure sections for the quilt-top pieces, borders, and backing, if necessary. Save the longest lengths of fabric for borders, so they will not have to be pieced from short lengths. When cutting the fabric for borders, you may want to cut them slightly longer than the directions call for.

Especially on a patchwork top, borders may require a bit of extra fabric if the width of your seams varies during stitching, causing the quilt top to be slightly larger than planned.

Patchwork Tops. All the patchwork quilts in this book have straight seams and can be stitched on a sewing machine. A basic knowledge of plain sewing, with accuracy and neatness, is all that's required for constructing these quilt tops.

All seams must be even. A ¼″ seam allowance is suggested in the instructions, and it must always be consistent. Use the pressure foot on the sewing machine as a ¼″ stitching guide. A piece of masking tape placed on the machine's needle plate also works well as a guide. If you choose a wider or narrower seam allowance, the width must be maintained consistently.

Pressing as you go is one of the most important steps in making an exquisite quilt top, and one that should never be passed by. It is almost impossible to join seams, matching their corners, unless they are pressed with care. Each seam must be pressed to one side, usually onto the darker fabric. Pressing the dark seams onto the dark blocks will eliminate any shadows that might show through the fabric. Do not try to press the seams open, since this only lessens the strength of the seam. If there are protruding angles of fabric — especially triangular-shaped pieces — at the end of a seam, they can be trimmed as you stitch. The less fabric there is to bunch up underneath the seam, the smoother the finished quilt top will be.

Before stitching the pieces of the quilt top together, plan the layout and group the pieces so they form units that can be stitched into rows spanning the full length or width of the quilt. Most simply constructed patchwork tops are set together by joining the blocks into vertical rows and then joining the rows together to form the finished top. Quilts with diamond-shaped blocks are assembled in a similar way and are set in diagonal rows that are then assembled.

Some of the patchwork tops consist of blocks set together with mullion strips. The word *mullion* is taken from the narrow strips of wood or metal between the panes of glass in a window. Mullion strips give an illusion that the quilt blocks are surrounded by a picture frame. The short strips in a mullion design can be added to the individual blocks first. The blocks and strips can then be assembled into long rows and finally joined together with long mullion strips. The intersecting seams of the mullion strips must be joined accurately. Take time to pin the matching seams before you stitch the strips in place.

Appliquéd Whole-Cloth Tops. Stitching appliqué strips or pieces cut from fabric to a whole-cloth quilt top is not difficult. First, all raw edges of the appliqué fabric must be turned under ¼″ and pressed. If the fabric does not hold the creases, secure the edges with basting stitches.

To center and place the appliqué pieces correctly, mark the center of the quilt top by pressing crease lines the length and width of the fabric with a warm iron. Using the crease lines for guides, arrange the pieces on the quilt top. Once you determine the layout, pin the pieces carefully in place.

If you prefer, the appliqué can be done by machine. Use a harmonizing thread and hold the stitching very close to the edge of the appliqué fabric. Of course, hand stitching is the best way to do appliqué. Hand appliqué can be done with a blind stitch, blanket stitch, whipstitch, or running stitch (see the illustrations).

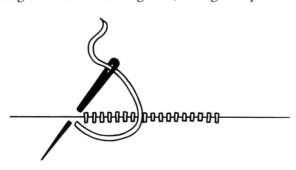

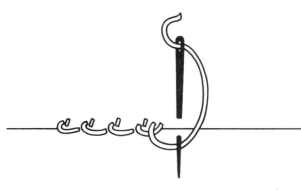

Blind stitch. Knot the end of a single strand of thread. Pull the needle up from the underside of the background fabric, then push it through and out the folded edge of the appliqué. Reinsert the needle into the background fabric, pointing it straight down from the folded edge. Make the next stitch by coming up from the background fabric ¹⁄₁₆″ to the left of the first stitch.

Blanket stitch. This decorative stitch can be used for appliqué or embroidery. Knot together one end of two or three strands of embroidery floss. Pull the needle up from the underside of the background fabric near the edge of the appliqué. Hold the thread under your thumb against the background fabric and form a loop to the left of the needle. Put the needle through the appliqué ¼″ from the edge, then pull it up through the background fabric at the edge of the appliqué, passing the needle through the looped thread.

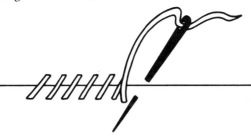

Whipstitch. Pull a knotted, single strand of thread up through the background fabric and pierce both layers of the folded edge of the appliqué. Reinsert the needle into the background fabric, making small slanted stitches along the edge of the appliqué.

Running stitch. This stitch can be used as a decorative stitch and a quilting stitch. Small, evenly spaced stitches ¹⁄₁₆″ long worked close to the edge of the appliqué will keep the fabric in place.

Assembling a Quilt

The finishing touch for any quilt is the hand quilting, which is not only decorative but also secures the three layers — the top, batting, and backing — that form the quilt. Most of the quilts in this book call for outline quilting around the stenciled design. If other parts of the quilt top will be quilted, the quilting design should be marked very lightly on the quilt top before it's basted to the batting and backing.

Templates. Quilting, or window, templates are often used to transfer a quilting design to a quilt top. These are made from Mylar or cardboard in much the same way as a stencil, and designs are reproduced on the quilt top by tracing around the opening. Quilting designs can also be transferred by tracing around shapes cut from cardboard, sandpaper, or firm plastic. When transferring a design, mark it very lightly with a No. 3 (hard) lead pencil or dressmaker's marking pencil. Some quilters prefer to mark quilting designs with a water-soluble marking pen made specifically for use on fabrics. Any remaining lines from the pen can be removed easily with a damp cloth. Other marking implements include tailor's chalk or a sliver of soap. Whatever marker you choose, test it first to be sure it can easily be removed from the fabric.

Intricate quilting designs can be transferred to the quilt top by the use of tough, transparent perforated paper. Perforated quilting designs can be purchased in craft supply stores, or they can be made by tracing a design on a sheet of Mylar and machine stitching without thread along the lines. To transfer the design to the quilt top, dip a piece of cotton into a saucer of cornstarch (for dark fabrics) or cinnamon (for light fabrics), and rub the powder gently over the perforations.

Other Supplies. The short needles used for quilting are known as "betweens" or quilting needles and come in sizes 7, 8, 9, and 10. The larger the number, the shorter the needle. Practice will reduce awkwardness with the short quilting needle; those who prefer sewing with a thinner needle might try a "sharp," a slender needle with a larger eye. The use of a thimble is essential for good quilting.

Quilting thread has a waxed surface and is made of strong, thick cotton. It comes in a wide selection of colors, so it should not be difficult to choose a color that harmonizes with the fabric of the quilt top. A large quilt will require two spools of quilting thread, and a small quilt will need one spool. Beginning quilters should learn to knot the end of the thread that is cut from the spool, which will ensure smoother sewing and easier handling of the thread.

Polyester thread is not recommended as a substitute for quilting thread. The properties of polyester fibers cause the threads to stretch and tangle too frequently to be satisfactory for quilting.

Lap quilting hoops are available in craft and needlework stores, and there is much to recommend their use. With a hoop, the quilter has the option to quilt almost anywhere and is no longer confined to a room where an old-fashioned floor quilting frame is set up. Some quilters even attribute the revival of quiltmaking in the 1970s and 1980s to the use of the hoop. A 14" round hoop is best suited for lap quilting.

Basting. Before quilting with a lap hoop can begin, the three layers of the quilt must be basted together. Give the quilt top and backing a final pressing to remove all wrinkles. Locate the center of the quilt backing by folding the fabric in quarters, then place a safety pin in the center. Next, spread the quilt backing, wrong side up, on a large flat surface. A Ping-Pong table is ideal.

The surface of the table must be protected because the needle will cause scratches during the basting process.

Place the batting on top of the quilt backing, smoothing out all wrinkles. Find the center of the quilt top and mark it with a safety pin. With the right side up, place the quilt top on the batting, matching the two center points where the safety pins are located. Square up all four corners to make the backing and quilt top even. Use many safety pins to secure the layers.

Thread a large darning needle with regular thread, but do not knot it. Beginning at the center of the quilt, baste to the outer edges, making a large X from corner to corner (see the illustration). Then baste vertical rows not more than 8" apart, starting near the center of the quilt and working rows out to the edge. Baste around the outer edge of the quilt. Trim the batting, leaving not more than a 2" overhang. The quilt is now ready for hand quilting, which is always begun in the center of the quilt.

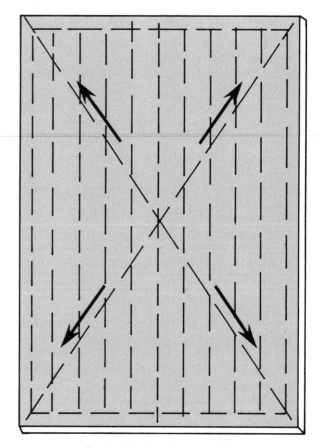

Basting the three layers together.

Quilting. Proper placement of the lap hoop on the section to be quilted is very important. Place the design to be worked on within the hoop, and clamp the hoop shut. After setting the hoop, turn it over so that the back of the quilt faces up. Carefully release the hoop and smooth the quilt backing. Reset the hoop and turn it to the front side again. Careful handling of this detail will eliminate wrinkles on both sides and ensure a taut quilting surface that will be much easier to sew.

Once the hoop is set, everything within the hoop should be quilted. If the design extends beyond the area of the hoop, many threaded needles can be used at one time on different parts of the design. With this procedure, you will not have to cut the thread when you reach the edge of the hoop, and a continuous flow of quilting can be maintained. Leave the threaded needles in the quilt when you reach the edge of the hoop, and bury the points of the needles in the batting to safeguard against needle pricks. Reset the hoop, and continue the quilting on the next part of the design. When not in use, the hoop should be removed from the quilt to prevent the fabric from stretching.

It is not difficult to master the quilting, or running, stitch (see page 45). Cut the thread on a slant to make easy work of threading the needle. Thread the needle, knot the newly cut end of the thread, and insert the needle into the quilt top near a seam or near the edge of a stenciled design. Pull the thread and knot into the batting, then come up where the quilting is to start. No knots should show on the front or back of the quilt (see the illustration).

Sewing from right to left, take a small backstitch and then push the needle straight down through the three layers of the quilt while slightly lifting the quilt with the fingers of your left hand, which is underneath the quilt. Your fingers will feel the needle prick with each stitch. Take three or four stitches through all layers, then pull the thread through the quilt.

When quilting along the seams, keep the quilting lines very close to the seam, though not actually on top of it. Avoid quilting along the side of the seam where the seam allowance is pressed since it can be quite difficult to pass the needle through four thicknesses of fabric plus the batting. Outline quilting should be held close to the edge of painted parts of the stenciled design.

Concentrate on making uniform stitches on the back of the quilt as well as the top so the quilt will look good when reversed. With practice, you'll develop a sense of rhythm that will produce small, even stitches. Quilting by hand does take time and patience, but this is the part of the American quiltmaking tradition that's most worth preserving.

Tying. Tying off a quilt with yarn is a quick way to secure the layers or give a decorative touch to the quilt top. Tying is done with wool yarn — knots made with wool are more secure and do not slip as do those made with synthetic yarn.

To tie off a quilt, thread a long, sharp, large-eyed needle with one or two strands of yarn. (Double strands

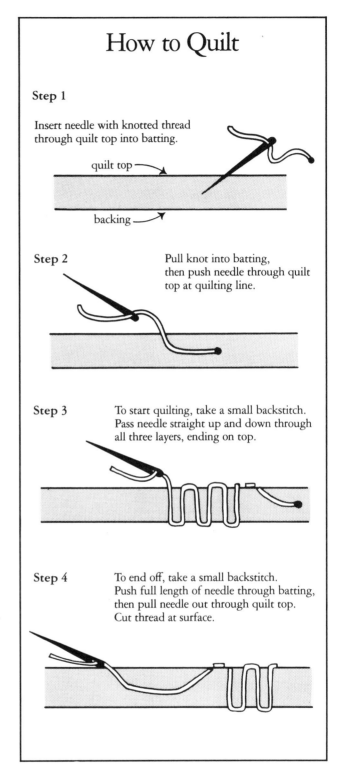

How to Quilt

Step 1

Insert needle with knotted thread through quilt top into batting.

quilt top →

backing →

Step 2

Pull knot into batting, then push needle through quilt top at quilting line.

Step 3

To start quilting, take a small backstitch. Pass needle straight up and down through all three layers, ending on top.

Step 4

To end off, take a small backstitch. Push full length of needle through batting, then pull needle out through quilt top. Cut thread at surface.

of yarn will give a flower-like appearance to the knot.) Push the needle through all three layers to the back side of the quilt, leaving about 4″ of yarn on the top. Bring the needle back through to the top, making a ¼″ stitch in the backing. Tie a square knot on the top side and trim the ends, leaving 1″ tails of yarn. To prevent the batting from shifting when the quilt is washed, ties should be placed no farther than 4″ apart.

Finishing a Quilt

Edges. When the quilting or tying is completed, trim all batting even with the quilt top and backing. If the same fabric was used for the backing and the top, the edges of the backing and the batting can be folded over to the top side of the quilt and hemmed down. If the backing fabric does not match or blend with the fabric of the quilt top, the edges of the top and the batting should be folded over to the back of the quilt and hemmed.

Starting in the middle of each edge of the quilt and working toward the corners, fold all three layers under ¼″, then fold over again about 1″ to form the finished edge (see the illustration). Fold the side edges first, then the top and bottom edges. Pin the folds in place, using many straight pins, and hem. The edges will be plump, forming a nice outer finish to the quilt.

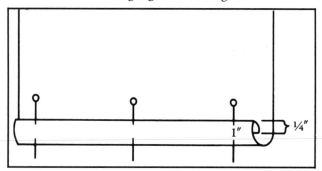

Folding edges for hemming.

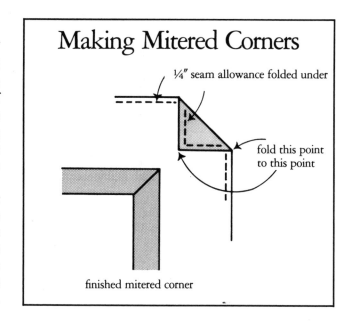

Making Mitered Corners

¼″ seam allowance folded under

fold this point to this point

finished mitered corner

Corners. If the corners are to be bound in a square fashion, trim away ½″ of batting for about 1″ along the top and bottom edges of the quilt at each corner (see the illustration). First fold the two side edges of the quilt toward the center, and pin. Then fold the top and bottom edges of the quilt over the folded sides, and pin. Hem all edges neatly.

The mitered method also makes a pleasing corner for a quilt. When you're ready to finish the edges, turn under a ¼″ seam allowance on the edges leading to the

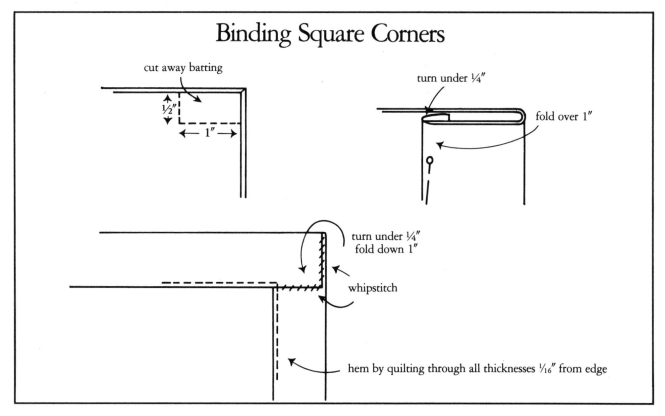

Binding Square Corners

cut away batting

½″

1″

turn under ¼″

fold over 1″

turn under ¼″
fold down 1″

whipstitch

hem by quilting through all thicknesses ¹⁄₁₆″ from edge

Selecting a Quilt: For Novices to Experts

Beginning

Christmas Rose of Sharon
Circle of Tulips
Creeping Periwinkle
Dutch Tulips
Holly Wreath
Laurel Leaf
Leaf and Chain
Oak Leaf and Reel
Peter Rabbit
Rose of Sharon
Rose Wreath and Bud
Rose Wreath with Tulips
Running Rabbits
Song Birds
Teddy Bear
True Oak Leaves
Whig Rose
Wild Rose

Intermediate

American Tulip
Birds of a Feather
Blue Whig Rose
Country Chickens
Hearts and Flowers
Hearts and More Hearts
Pineapple
Scotch Thistle
Sweetheart
Turkey Tracks
Whirl of Maple Leaves

Advanced

Art Deco
Art Nouveau
Christmas Star
Theorem Theme
Victorian Crazy Quilt

corners. Fold the corner of the quilt over to where the hem will come, creating a triangular shape. Trim away any excess batting. Bring both sides of the folded corner together, and hem along the diagonal seam (see the illustration).

Although none of the quilts in this book are bound with bias, a bias strip of fabric may also be used to finish the edges. Bias binding for quilts can be purchased at sewing goods stores.

When the edges are finished, proudly sign your name and date on the quilt. Perhaps a dedication is in order. This finishing touch is lasting and can be as sentimental as you wish.

Caring for a Quilt

A hand-stenciled quilt is a delicate work of art and should be treated with care to ensure that it becomes an heirloom to be handed down from one generation to another. Laundering can be the single most important factor in preserving a quilt and should be done with extreme care.

Fill a bathtub with warm water, add ¾ cup of mild liquid detergent, such as Ivory Liquid or Woolite, and place the quilt in the water. Agitate the quilt very gently by hand until it looks clean. Leave the quilt in the tub and drain out the water. Refill the tub with warm water and rinse the quilt several times if necessary until the water is clean. After the last draining of the tub, carefully squeeze the water from the quilt. You can also place the quilt between towels and squeeze to extract the water. Do not twist or wring the quilt.

If the quilt is not too heavy, it can be placed in a washer and set on the spin dry cycle. Do not attempt this if your washer is not a heavy-duty machine; instead, dry the quilt on a flat surface on top of a clean sheet. Do not dry a quilt in the sun or on a clothesline. Never attempt to iron a quilt.

The clean quilt should not be stored in a plastic bag, which could trap moisture and cause mildew. A quilt should be loosely rolled up in a clean sheet and placed on a long shelf for storage. Acids in wood can discolor fabric, so avoid direct contact of a quilt with wood.

Of course, the best way to "store" your quilt is to display it. If its color scheme or size is not just right for using it on a bed, you can easily use the quilt as a wall hanging. Hand stitch a sleeve or casing along the full length of the upper edge of the quilt backing, and insert a dowel as long as the casing. This will ensure that the weight of the quilt is evenly distributed. Screw-eye hooks can be placed at each end of the dowel. Display the quilt on a wall where sunlight will not shine directly upon it. ♡

WILD ROSE
(color plate 1)

Patchwork Quilt with Stenciled Blocks
39" x 53"

Materials

quilt-top layout

▷ 3 yards of 40"-wide unbleached muslin for quilt-top blocks, border, and backing

▷ 1½ yards of 36"-wide peach cotton fabric for mullion strips and border

▷ Quilt batting, crib size

▷ 2 (11"-square) sheets of frosted Mylar

▷ X-acto-type knife for cutting stencils

▷ Piece of glass for cutting base

▷ 1 (No. 4) stiff, round stencil brush

▷ Cadmium orange acrylic paint, or any color that harmonizes with fabric

▷ Chromium oxide green acrylic paint

Cutting and Piecing

All fabric must be washed and ironed. Trim selvage edges.

Cut six 11½"-square blocks from the muslin.

Cut eight 3½" x 11½" strips and three 3½" x 45½" strips from the peach fabric for the mullions. Piece four short mullion strips to three large blocks, making a vertical row. Repeat for three remaining large blocks. Piece the long mullion strips to these two rows (see the layout).

Cut two 2½" x 35½" strips and two 2½" x 45½" strips from the muslin for a border.

Cut two 3½" x 41½" strips and two 3½" x 49½" strips from the peach fabric for a second border.

Add the muslin border around the mullions, and finish by adding the outer peach border.

Place one sheet of Mylar on the Wild Rose stencil pattern on the following page, and trace just the flowers. Trace the leaves and stems on the other piece of Mylar. Be sure to mark the top on both stencil sheets to register the stencils correctly when painting. Cut the stencils on the glass.

Paint each of the six 11" muslin blocks, using the flower stencil first, then the leaf stencil. Be certain to center the stencils on each block.

Allow the paint to dry overnight, and set with a hot, dry iron. Use a pressing cloth to avoid scorching.

Assembling and Finishing

Mark the quilting design below on the mullion strips and borders with a No. 3 (hard) lead pencil or dressmaker's marking pencil.

Layer the backing, batting, and top. Baste together.

Outline quilt all parts of the stenciled design. Quilt along the seams around the stenciled blocks, and quilt the penciled-in design lines on the mullions and borders.

To finish the edges, bring the top material and batting to the back side, fold under to make a 1" hem, and pin. Hem to the quilt backing. ♡

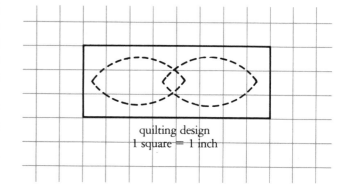

quilting design
1 square = 1 inch

SWEETHEART
(color plate 2)

Whole-Cloth Quilt with Appliqué and Stenciled Design
69″ x 86″

Materials

▷ 2 twin-size white polyester/cotton–blend bed sheets for quilt top and backing

▷ 2½ yards of 45″-wide deep rose muslin for appliqué and border

▷ Quilt batting, twin size

▷ 2 (9″-square) pieces of cardboard

▷ 1 (18″ x 24″) sheet of frosted Mylar (cut into smaller sections as necessary)

▷ X-acto-type knife for cutting stencils

▷ Piece of glass for cutting base

▷ 1 (No. 4) stiff, round stencil brush

▷ Deep magenta acrylic paint, or any color that harmonizes with fabric

▷ White acrylic paint for mixing pastel colors

Cutting and Piecing

All fabric must be washed and ironed. Trim selvage edges.

Cut four 3″ x 40″ strips from the rose fabric to make a 34″-square picture frame (outside measurements). Join the four strips by mitering corners (see the diagram at right). Turn under ¼″ on all sides and press.

Fold the quilt-top fabric in quarters. Press folds with a warm iron. These crease lines will act as guidelines in centering the rose-fabric frame. Place the frame in a diamond position on the quilt top. Pin in place. With matching thread, machine stitch very close to edge of rose fabric.

Cut four 3″ x 48″ strips from the rose fabric to make a second frame. Miter the corners for the top and bottom of the frame (see the photo). Turn under ¼″ on all sides and press. Place the strips on the quilt top 8″ away from the center frame. Pin in place and topstitch by machine very close to the edge of the strips.

Make an 8″ cardboard template by enlarging the heart pattern on the following page, and cut eight rose fabric hearts.

Cut a cardboard heart ¼″ smaller than the cloth hearts. Place this cardboard heart on top of a cloth heart and press a ¼″ seam allowance over onto the cardboard. Repeat for each cloth heart. Place the hearts on the quilt top, four in the center frame and one in each corner of the quilt top. Pin and machine stitch very close to the edge of each heart.

Cut two 5″ x 71½″ strips and two 5″ x 79½″ strips from the rose fabric for a final border. Stitch in place.

Cut the Mylar, place one piece on the love dove and heart stencil patterns on the following page, and trace. Trace the stencil patterns for the bowknots and heart borders (see page 129 in the Portfolio section) on a second piece of Mylar. Cut the stencils on the glass.

Place the stencils as desired on the quilt top. Use the deep magenta paint full strength for the heart borders and in accent areas on the doves and bowknots. Add white paint to make a contrasting pastel for the light pink hearts (stenciled on the appliquéd hearts) and for the other areas on the doves and bowknots.

Allow the paint to dry overnight, and set with a hot, dry iron. Use a pressing cloth to avoid scorching.

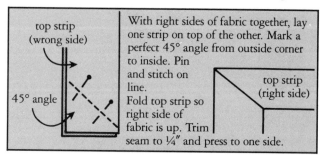

Assembling and Finishing

Using a No. 3 (hard) lead pencil or dressmaker's marking pencil, lightly mark heart quilting designs on the quilt top by tracing around the stencil used for painting the light pink hearts.

Layer the backing, batting, and top. Baste together.

Outline quilt the love dove stencils. Quilt along the seams where the rose fabric has been appliquéd, and quilt the penciled-in design lines.

Finish the edges by bringing the backing material and batting to the front of the quilt. Fold under to make a 1″ hem, and pin. Hem to the quilt top. ♡

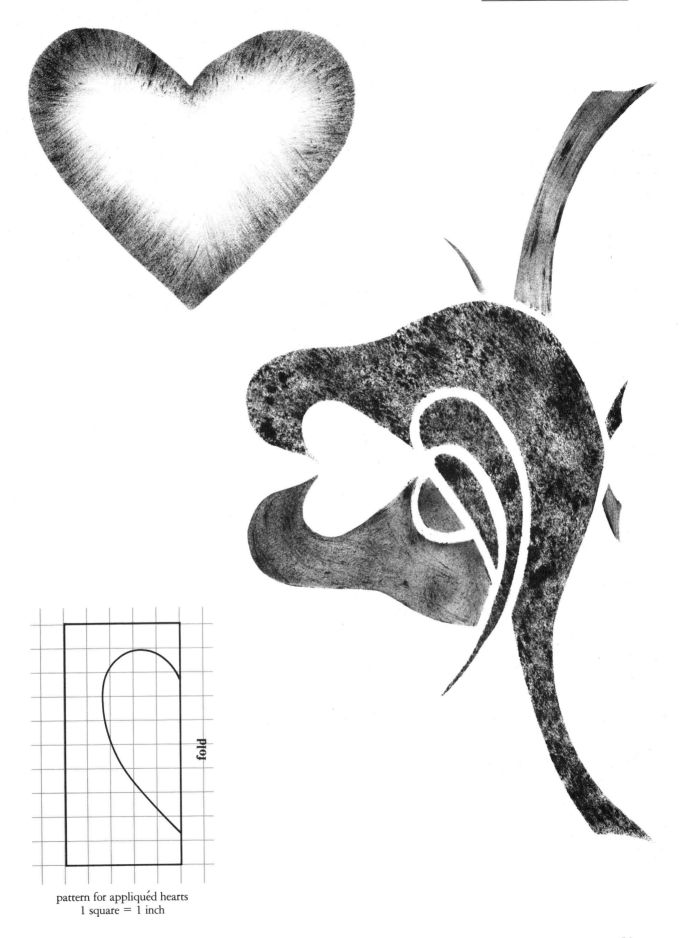

pattern for appliquéd hearts
1 square = 1 inch

fold

SCOTCH THISTLE

(color plate 3)

Patchwork Quilt with Stenciled Blocks

56″ x 78″

Materials

▷ 2 twin-size white polyester/cotton–blend bed sheets for quilt-top blocks and backing

▷ 3 yards of 36″-wide light gray calico print for quilt-top blocks and border

▷ Quilt batting, twin size

▷ 1 (8″-square) sheet of frosted Mylar

▷ X-acto-type knife for cutting stencils

▷ Piece of glass for cutting base

▷ 1 (No. 4) stiff, round stencil brush

▷ Black acrylic paint

Cutting and Piecing

All fabric must be washed and ironed. Trim selvage edges.

Cut twenty-eight 6½″-square white blocks.

To make 22 triangular pieces, cut 22 additional 6½″-square white blocks. Draw a diagonal line across the center of each block, add a ¼″ seam allowance along the diagonal, and cut; discard the smaller piece. Repeat for remaining blocks.

To make four smaller triangular pieces, cut four additional 6½″-square white blocks. Draw an X from corner to corner across each block, dividing it into quarters. Add a ¼″ seam allowance on two sides of one quarter, and cut; discard the remaining piece. Repeat for remaining blocks.

Cut forty 6½″-square blocks from the gray calico.

Piece the 6½″-square white blocks and 6½″-square gray blocks as shown in the layout, alternating colors and arranging them in a diagonal, diamond-like pattern. You should have five gray blocks across and eight gray blocks down, and four white blocks across and seven white blocks down. Piece the 22 large triangular pieces into the spaces on the outer edges. Use the four small triangular pieces for the corners.

Cut two 6½″ x 58½″ strips and two 8½″ x 68½″ strips from the gray calico for a border. Add the 8½″-wide gray strips to the long sides, and add the 6½″-wide gray strips to the top and bottom. Press all seams away from the white blocks and onto the gray blocks.

Place the Mylar on the thistle pattern on the following page, and trace. Cut the stencil on the glass.

With black paint, stencil paint only the full-size white blocks.

Allow the paint to dry overnight, and set with a hot, dry iron. Use a pressing cloth to avoid scorching.

quilt-top layout

Assembling and Finishing

Quilting can be added to the calico blocks, if desired; use the quilting design on the following page. Mark all quilting lines with a No. 3 (hard) lead pencil or dressmaker's marking pencil.

Layer the backing, batting, and top. Baste together.

Because of the delicacy of the thistle design, it is best not to use outline quilting. Quilting the thistle blocks ½″ away from the seams is sufficient.

To finish the edges, bring the backing material and batting to the front of the quilt, fold them under to create a 1″ white hem, and pin. Hem to the quilt top. ♡

quilting design
1 square = 1 inch

AMERICAN TULIP

(color plate 4)

Patchwork Quilt with Stenciled Blocks

47″ x 68″

Materials

▷ 6 yards of 36″-wide unbleached muslin for quilt-top blocks, border, and backing

▷ 3 yards of 36″-wide blue calico print for quilt-top blocks and borders

▷ 2 yards of 40″-wide red cotton fabric for borders

▷ Quilt batting, twin size

▷ 1 (12″-square) sheet of frosted Mylar

▷ X-acto-type knife for cutting stencils

▷ Piece of glass for cutting base

▷ 1 (No. 4) stiff, round stencil brush

▷ Cadmium red medium acrylic paint

▷ Cobalt blue acrylic paint

Cutting and Piecing

All fabric must be washed and ironed. Trim selvage edges.

Cut six 11½″-square blocks from the muslin.

Cut twelve 13½″-square blocks from the blue calico. Two of these blocks will be used full size. To make six triangular pieces from six of the blocks, draw a diagonal line across the center of a block, add a ¼″ seam allowance along the diagonal, and cut; discard the smaller piece. Repeat with five blocks.

To make four small triangular pieces from four full-size blocks, draw an X from corner to corner across a block, dividing it in quarters. Add a ¼″ seam allowance on two sides of one quarter, and cut; discard the remaining piece. Repeat with three blocks.

Cut twelve 1½″ x 11½″ strips and twelve 1½″ x 13½″ strips from the blue calico to frame the six muslin blocks. Piece two short and two long strips to each block.

Cut twelve 1½″ x 13½″ strips and twelve 1½″ x 15½″ strips from the red cotton fabric to frame the blue strips. Piece two short and two long strips to each framed muslin block.

Cut four 1½″ x 13½″ strips and twenty 1½″ x 15½″ strips from the muslin to frame the blue calico blocks (see the color plate). Stitch two 13½″ strips

and two 15½″ strips to each full-size block. Stitch the 15½″ strips to the two short sides of each large triangle and to the long side of each small triangle. Extend the strips a bit beyond the triangles — the excess can be cut off later.

Stitch the large blocks together as shown in the photo, alternating blocks and arranging them in a diamond pattern, with two muslin blocks across and three down. The two large blue calico blocks will be in the center, and the blue calico triangles will fill in on the sides and corners.

Cut two 1½″ x 43½″ strips and two 1½″ x 66½″ strips from the red fabric for a border around all the assembled blocks. Stitch in place.

Cut two 1½″ x 47½″ strips and two 1½″ x 66½″ strips from the muslin for a second border. Stitch in place.

Cut two 1½″ x 49½″ strips and two 1½″ x 68½″ strips from the blue calico for the final border. Stitch in place.

Place the Mylar on the American Tulip design on the following page, and trace. Cut the stencil on the glass.

The stencil will be used for painting two colors, so first cover the blue sections of the stencil (see the photo) with masking tape. Center the stencil on an unbleached muslin block and paint the red flowers and the center design. Remove the masking tape from the stencil when all the red painting is finished. Tape the red part of the stencil, and proceed with the blue stencil painting.

Allow the paint to dry overnight, and set with a hot, dry iron. Use a pressing cloth to avoid scorching.

Assembling and Finishing

Using the Mylar stencil as a quilting template, mark the tulip design on the blue calico blocks and triangles with a No. 3 (hard) lead pencil or dressmaker's marking pencil.

Layer the backing, batting, and top. Baste together.

Quilt the penciled-in design lines. Quilt along the seams, and outline quilt all parts of the stenciled design.

To finish the edges, bring the top material and batting to the back side, fold under to make a 1″ hem, and pin. Hem to the quilt backing. ♡

CHRISTMAS STAR
(color plate 5)

Advanced

Whole-Cloth Quilt with Appliqué and Stenciled Design
67″ x 95″

Materials

▷ 2 twin-size white polyester/cotton–blend bed sheets for quilt top and backing

▷ 4 yards of 36″-wide red-and-white striped fabric for appliqué and border

▷ Quilt batting, queen size

▷ ¼ (3½ oz.) skein of 4-ply bright red wool yarn

▷ 1 (7″-square) piece of cardboard

▷ 1 (8″-square) sheet of frosted Mylar

▷ X-acto-type knife for cutting stencils

▷ Piece of glass for cutting base

▷ 1 (No. 4) stiff, round stencil brush

▷ Hooker's green acrylic paint

Cutting and Piecing

All fabric must be washed and ironed. Trim selvage edges.

Make a cardboard template from the pattern for the five-pointed Christmas star on the following page.

Using the template, cut 130 pieces from the red-and-white striped fabric, making sure the stripes of the fabric follow the direction on the pattern. The stripes must match where the pieces are joined together.

Join ten pieces together, forming a circle with an open star in the center. Make 13 of these star circles.

Press under ¼″ seam allowance on the inside and outside of each star circle. Baste.

Arrange the circles on the quilt top (see the layout), allowing 9″ between the closest parts of each two circles. Pin each circle in place, and hand appliqué to the quilt-top fabric. Be sure all the stars are aligned with one another.

Cut two 4″ x 69″ strips and two 4″ x 90″ strips from the striped fabric to make a border around the entire quilt. (If your quilt top is smaller or larger than the size given here, measure it for the border.) Stitch in place.

Place the Mylar on the pine tree stencil pattern on the following page, and trace. Cut the stencil on the glass.

Position the stencil at the outer edge of a star circle, butting the tree trunk against a seam of the circle. Stencil paint a pine tree at each of the ten seams. The trees should follow the direction of the circle seams so that the trees seem to radiate from the center of the star. Stencil trees around all of the star circles.

Allow the paint to dry overnight, and set with a hot, dry iron. Use a pressing cloth to avoid scorching.

quilt-top layout

Assembling and Finishing

Layer the backing, batting, and top. Baste together.

Quilt around each star circle, ¼″ from the edge of the circle. Quilt inside each circle, ¼″ from the inner part of the star shape. Outline quilt all the pine tree stencils.

Place a 1″ tie of red wool yarn at the top of each pine tree and one in the center of each star circle.

To finish the edges, bring the backing material and batting to the top side, fold under, and pin, forming a 1″ white border. Hem to the quilt top.   ♡

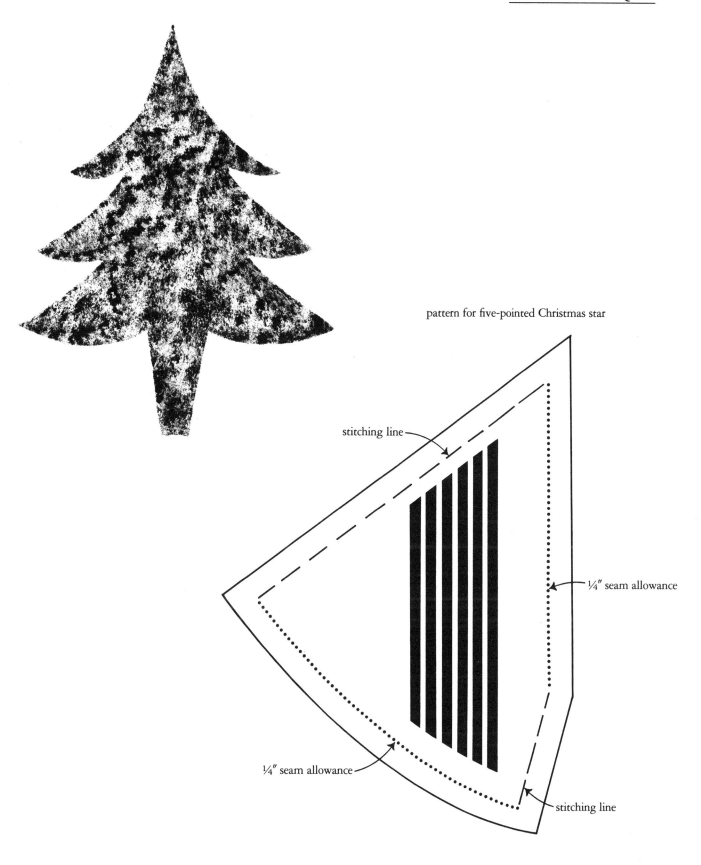

pattern for five-pointed Christmas star

stitching line

¼″ seam allowance

¼″ seam allowance

stitching line

COUNTRY CHICKENS

(color plate 6)

Intermediate

Patchwork Quilt with Stenciled Blocks

65″ x 85″

Materials

▷ 2 twin-size light blue polyester/cotton-blend bed sheets for quilt-top blocks, borders, and backing

▷ 3 yards of 36″-wide blue calico print for mullions and border

▷ Quilt batting, twin size

▷ ¼ (3½ oz.) skein of 4-ply black wool yarn

▷ 4 (9″ x 12″) sheets of frosted Mylar

▷ X-acto-type knife for cutting stencils

▷ Piece of glass for cutting base

▷ 1 (No. 4) stiff, round stencil brush

▷ Cerulean blue acrylic paint, or any color that harmonizes with calico print

▷ Black acrylic paint

▷ Cadmium red light acrylic paint

Cutting and Piecing

All fabric must be washed and ironed. Trim selvage edges.

Cut forty-eight 7½″ x 10½″ blocks from one light blue sheet. Reserve a long strip of the sheet for the borders.

Cut ninety-six 2″ x 10½″ strips from the blue calico for mullion strips. Piece the strips to the long sides of the light blue blocks. Each block will now have three pieces — two calico strips and one light blue block.

Piece the blocks together, alternating the positions of the calico strips horizontally and vertically (see the color plate). Piece six blocks across and eight blocks down.

Cut two 2″ x 63½″ strips and two 2″ x 80½″ strips from the blue calico to form a border around all blocks. Stitch in place.

Cut two 2½″ x 67½″ strips and two 2½″ x 83½″ strips from the light blue fabric for a final border. Stitch in place.

Place one sheet of Mylar on the chicken stencil pattern on the following page, and trace just the body. Trace the body of the second chicken pattern (see page 131 in the Portfolio section) on a second sheet of Mylar. Trace the comb and feather lines for each chicken stencil on a separate sheet of Mylar. Cut the stencils on the glass.

Stencil paint the chicken bodies with the blue paint. Use the tall chicken on the vertical blocks and the short chicken on the horizontal blocks. Do not try to paint the bodies solidly. Give a variegated effect by mixing a little black paint into the blue paint and allowing the blue background of the fabric to show through. If necessary, practice this technique before you stencil the quilt top.

Place the comb and feather stencils over the painted chicken bodies, and paint the combs red and the feather lines black.

Allow the paint to dry overnight, and set with a hot, dry iron. Use a pressing cloth to avoid scorching.

Assembling and Finishing

Layer the backing, batting, and top. Baste together.

Quilt along the seams around all blocks.

Add 1″ ties of black wool yarn in the center of the blue mullion strips around each stenciled block (see the photo).

To finish the edges, bring the top material and batting to the back side, fold under to make a 1″ hem, and pin. Hem to the quilt backing. ♡

BIRDS OF A FEATHER
(color plate 7)

Patchwork Quilt with Stenciled Blocks

41″ x 55″

Materials

▷ 1 twin-size white polyester/cotton–blend bed sheet for quilt-top blocks, border, and backing

▷ 2 yards of 36″-wide light blue cotton fabric for mullions and border

▷ Quilt batting, crib size

▷ 1 (5″ x 8″) sheet of frosted Mylar

▷ 1 (14″-square) sheet of frosted Mylar

▷ X-acto-type knife for cutting stencils

▷ Piece of glass for cutting base

▷ 1 (No. 4) stiff, round stencil brush

▷ 1 (8″-square) piece of metal window screen

▷ Chromium oxide green acrylic paint

▷ Cobalt blue acrylic paint

▷ Cadmium red medium acrylic paint

▷ White acrylic paint to lighten the red paint

▷ Burnt umber acrylic paint

Cutting and Piecing

All fabric must be washed and ironed. Trim selvage edges.

Cut six 10½″-square blocks from the white sheet.

Cut four 4½″ x 10½″ strips and three 4½″ x 38½″ strips from the light blue fabric to frame the white blocks. Piece two of the short strips to three blocks, making a vertical row. Repeat with the remaining short strips and blocks. Piece the three long strips to the vertical rows.

Cut two 4½″ x 32½″ strips from the light blue fabric for the top and bottom mullions. Stitch in place.

Cut two 4½″ x 40½″ strips and two 4½″ x 46½″ strips from the white sheet for a border around the blue mullions. Stitch in place. The remaining half of the white sheet will be used for the quilt backing.

Cut two 2″ x 43½″ strips and two 2″ x 54½″ strips from the light blue fabric for the final border. Stitch in place.

Place the 14″-square sheet of Mylar on the bird pattern on the following page, and trace the tree and leaves only. Make a separate stencil for the birds in a corner of the Mylar sheet. Trace the pattern for the border design (see page 135, right, in the Portfolio section) on the 5″ x 8″ piece of Mylar. Cut the stencils on the glass.

When painting the bird stencil, cover the different color areas (see the photo) with masking tape. Stencil paint the green leaves first, including the ones on the border designs. Stencil paint the heads and wings of the birds blue. Carefully match up the stencil for the bird bodies with the painted head and wing sections. Stencil paint the bodies light pink.

Place the window screen over the tree section of the stencil, and paint the trees through the screen with burnt umber paint.

Allow the paint to dry overnight, and set with a hot, dry iron. Use a pressing cloth to avoid scorching.

Assembling and Finishing

Layer the backing, batting, and top. Baste together.

Outline quilt the entire stenciled bird design. Quilt ⅜″ away from all seams. Outline quilt the border design.

To finish the edges, bring the top material and batting to the back side, fold under to make a 1″ hem, and pin. Hem to the backing. ♡

WHIG ROSE

(cover and color plate 8)

Beginning

Patchwork Quilt with Stenciled Blocks

45″ x 59″

Materials

▷ 5 yards of 36″-wide unbleached muslin for quilt-top blocks, borders, and backing

▷ 2 yards of 36″-wide rose-colored cotton fabric for quilt-top blocks and borders

▷ Quilt batting, twin size

▷ 2 (12″-square) sheets of frosted Mylar

▷ X-acto-type knife for cutting stencils

▷ Piece of glass for cutting base

▷ 1 (No. 4) stiff, round stencil brush

▷ Chromium oxide green acrylic paint

▷ Deep magenta acrylic paint, or any color that harmonizes with the rose fabric

▷ White acrylic paint for mixing pastel colors

Cutting and Piecing

All fabric must be washed and ironed. Trim selvage edges.

Cut six 11½″-square blocks from the muslin.

Cut twelve 1½″ x 11½″ strips and twelve 1½″ x 13½″ strips from the rose fabric to frame the muslin squares. Stitch in place.

Cut thirty-six 3½″ x 4½″ blocks from the rose fabric. Cut twenty-four 2½″ x 4½″ blocks from the muslin. Piece these blocks on both sides of the muslin squares, alternating three rose and two muslin blocks on either side of the squares (see the quilt layout).

Cut eight 2″ x 21½″ strips from the muslin. Stitch the strips to the long sides of the pieced muslin/rose blocks, forming two rows of three blocks each (see the layout).

Cut one 1½″ x 45½″ strip from the rose fabric. Use this strip to join the two rows of pieced muslin/rose blocks.

Cut two 3½″ x 43½″ strips from the rose fabric for a top and bottom border. Stitch in place.

Cut two 3½″ x 43½″ strips from the muslin for a second border on the top and bottom. Stitch in place.

Cut two 2½″ x 47½″ strips and two 2½″ x 57½″ strips from the rose fabric for a final border. Stitch in place.

Place one sheet of Mylar on the Whig Rose stencil pattern on the following page, and trace just the leaves. Trace the flower on the second sheet of Mylar. Be sure to mark the top of each stencil to align the patterns. Cut the stencils on the glass.

Stencil paint the leaves green on the six large muslin blocks. Stencil paint the flowers in shades of pink, mixing the magenta paint with the white paint for the centers of the flowers. Line up both sheets of Mylar for accurate results.

Allow the paint to dry overnight, and set with a hot, dry iron. Use a pressing cloth to avoid scorching.

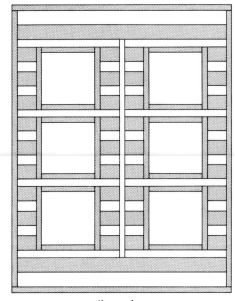

quilt-top layout

Assembling and Finishing

Using a 10″ dinner plate, mark a circle around each of the flowers with a No. 3 (hard) lead pencil or dressmaker's marking pencil. Using the oval quilting design on the following page, mark quilting lines on the borders and on the rose and unbleached muslin blocks around the large stenciled blocks.

Quilt along the seams, and outline quilt the entire stencil pattern. Quilt the penciled-in circles around the flowers and the oval shapes on the borders and on the rose and muslin blocks.

To finish the edges, bring the top material and batting to the back side, fold under to make a 1″ hem, and pin. Hem to the backing. ♡

quilting design
1 square = 1 inch

TEDDY BEAR

(color plate 9)

Whole-Cloth Quilt with Stenciled Design
40″ x 50″

Materials

▷ 1½ yards of 42″-wide small-dotted tan cotton fabric for quilt top

▷ 1½ yards of 42″-wide unbleached muslin for quilt backing

▷ Quilt batting, crib size

▷ 1 (9″-square) sheet of Mylar

▷ X-acto-type knife for cutting stencils

▷ Piece of glass for cutting base

▷ 1 (No. 4) stiff, round stencil brush

▷ Burnt sienna acrylic paint

▷ Yellow oxide acrylic paint

▷ Raw sienna acrylic paint

▷ Burnt umber acrylic paint

▷ Cadmium red light acrylic paint

Stenciling

All fabric must be washed and ironed. Trim selvage edges.

Place the Mylar on the Teddy Bear pattern on the following page, and trace. Cut the stencil on the glass.

Spend some time in planning a hit-and-miss layout for the teddy bears. Plan for a good repetition of the four different colors. In the quilt shown here, one row has four bears and the remaining five rows have five bears each, but this is only one of many possible layouts.

Cover the heart with masking tape, and stencil paint the bears. Move the masking tape, and paint the hearts red.

To add the finishing touch, draw in eyes and mouths and outline the noses and suspenders with a black laundry marker.

Allow the paint to dry overnight, and set with a hot, dry iron. Use a pressing cloth to avoid scorching.

Assembling and Finishing

Layer the backing, batting, and stenciled top. Baste together.

Outline quilt all the bears and the painted parts of the faces.

To add more interest to the background, quilt diagonally between the dots of the fabric. On the quilt shown in the photo, quilting rows are 1″ apart.

Finish the edges by bringing the top and batting to the back side. Fold under to make a 1″ hem, and pin. Hem to the backing.   ♡

HOLLY WREATH

(color plate 10)

Patchwork Quilt with Stenciled Blocks

48″ x 67″

Materials

▷ 1 twin-size white polyester/cotton–blend bed sheet for quilt-top blocks and backing

▷ 2 yards of 36″-wide bright red cotton fabric for mullions and border

▷ Quilt batting, twin size

▷ ¼ (3½ oz.) skein of 4-ply dark green wool yarn

▷ 1 (9″-square) sheet of frosted Mylar

▷ X-acto-type knife for cutting stencils

▷ Piece of glass for cutting base

▷ Leather or paper punch

▷ 1 (No. 4) stiff, round stencil brush

▷ Hooker's green acrylic paint

▷ Cadmium red medium acrylic paint

Cutting and Piecing

All fabric must be washed and ironed. Trim selvage edges.

Cut twenty-four 8″-square blocks from the white sheet.

Cut eighteen 2½″ x 8″ strips and five 2½″ x 36½″ strips from the red fabric for mullions. Piece three short strips to four white blocks, making a horizontal row. Repeat for five more rows. Piece the five long red mullion strips between the six rows.

Cut two 7½″ x 50½″ strips and two 7½″ x 55½″ strips from the red fabric for a border around the blocks. Stitch in place. Press all seams onto the red fabric.

Place the Mylar on the Holly Wreath pattern on the following page, and trace. Cut the stencil on the glass.

Use a leather punch to make berry holes in the stencil. You can also cut the holes by hand or with a paper punch.

Paint the green leaves first, being sure to cover the berry holes with masking tape. Then move the masking tape to the green leaves and stems near the berry holes, and paint the berries red.

Allow the paint to dry overnight, and set with a hot, dry iron. Use a pressing cloth to avoid scorching.

quilt-top layout

Assembling and Finishing

Layer the backing, batting, and top. Baste together.

Quilt along the seams around the white blocks.

Put 1″ ties of dark green wool yarn on the red mullion strips at the corners of the white blocks.

Finish the edges by bringing the backing material and batting to the front side. Fold under to make a 1″ hem, and pin. Hem to the quilt top. ♡

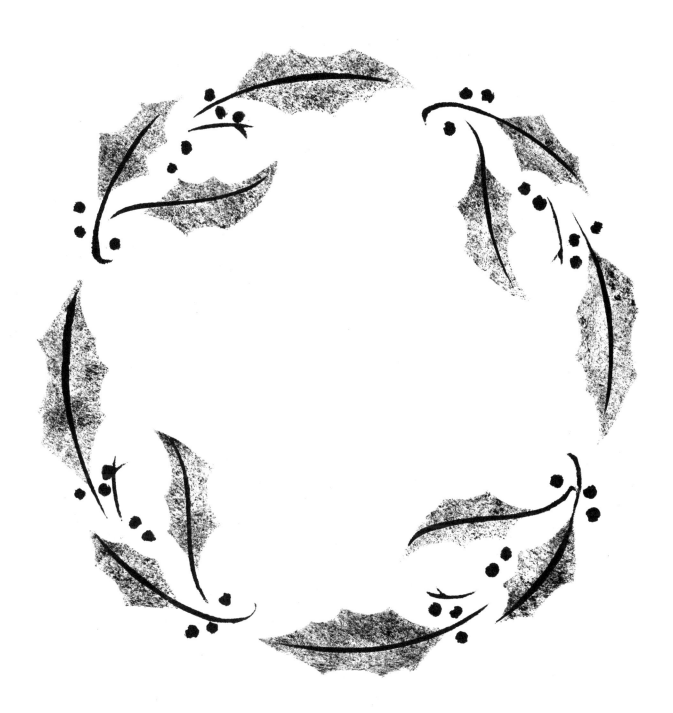

RUNNING RABBITS

(color plate 11)

Whole-Cloth Quilt with Stenciled Design

31″ x 50″

Materials

▷ 1½ yards of 36″-wide woven-check peach or yellow gingham for quilt top

▷ 1½ yards of 36″-wide unbleached muslin for quilt backing

▷ Quilt batting, crib size

▷ Newspaper (optional)

▷ 2 (5″ x 8″) sheets of frosted Mylar

▷ X-acto-type knife for cutting stencils

▷ Piece of glass for cutting base

▷ 1 (No. 4) stiff, round stencil brush

▷ Burnt sienna acrylic paint, or any color that harmonizes with a given color scheme

Stenciling

All fabric must be washed and ironed. Trim selvage edges.

Plan the layout of the design. If an oval layout is desired, cut a large oval from a double fold of newspaper, and mark the oval on the quilt top with a No. 3 (hard) lead pencil or dressmaker's marking pencil. Another, perhaps easier, way is to line up the stencil design along the lines of the woven gingham, creating a rectangle. Either method will produce good results.

Place the Mylar on the rabbit pattern on the following page, and trace only the rabbit. Trace the flowers and heart on the second sheet of Mylar. Cut the stencils on the glass.

Before you start to paint, check the layout of the design. When you're satisfied with it, proceed with the stencil painting.

Allow the paint to dry overnight, and set with a hot, dry iron. Use a pressing cloth to avoid scorching.

Assembling and Finishing

Mark oval quilting lines, if desired, on the quilt top (see the photo). Use a No. 3 (hard) lead pencil or dressmaker's marking pencil.

Layer the backing, batting, and top. Baste together.

Quilt around all parts of the stenciled design. Quilt along woven gingham lines or penciled-in oval design lines.

To finish the quilt, bring the top fabric and batting to the back side, fold under to make a 1″ hem, and pin. Hem to the backing. ♡

LEAF AND CHAIN
(color plate 12)

Patchwork Quilt with Stenciled Strips
52″ x 72″

Materials

▷ 6 yards of 36″-wide unbleached muslin for quilt top, border, and backing

▷ 3 yards of 36″-wide gold muslin for quilt top and border

▷ Quilt batting, twin size

▷ 1 (8″ x 12″) sheet of frosted Mylar

▷ X-acto-type knife for cutting stencils

▷ Piece of glass for cutting base

▷ 1 (No. 4) stiff, round stencil brush

▷ Burnt umber acrylic paint

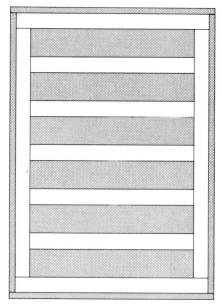

quilt-top layout

Cutting and Piecing

All fabric must be washed and ironed. Trim selvage edges.

Cut six 7½″ x 42½″ strips from the gold fabric.

Cut five 4½″ x 42½″ strips from the muslin.

Sew these 11 strips together, alternating colors and starting and ending with gold strips.

Cut two 4½″ x 50½″ strips and two 4½″ x 62½″ strips from the unbleached muslin for a border. Stitch in place.

Cut two 2½″ x 54½″ strips and two 2½″ x 70½″ strips from the gold fabric for the outer border. Stitch in place. Press all seams toward the gold fabric.

Place the Mylar on the Leaf and Chain pattern on the following page, and trace. Cut the stencil on the glass.

Plan the layout of the stencil pattern on the gold strips. Start the pattern at the center of a strip, and proceed toward the ends of the strip.

Stencil the pattern, starting at the center of each strip.

Allow the paint to dry overnight, and set with a hot, dry iron. Use a pressing cloth to avoid scorching.

Assembling and Finishing

Mark the quilting design below on the muslin strips and borders with a No. 3 (hard) lead pencil or dress-maker's marking pencil.

Layer the backing, batting, and quilt top. Baste all three layers together.

Quilt around just the stenciled chain. Quilt along the seams, and quilt the penciled-in design lines.

To finish the edges, bring the top fabric and batting to the back side of the quilt, turn under to make a 1″ hem, and pin. Hem to the backing. ♡

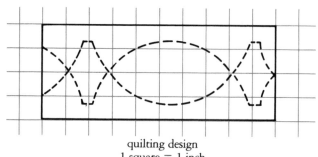

quilting design
1 square = 1 inch

VICTORIAN CRAZY QUILT
(color plate 13)

Advanced

Patchwork Quilt with Embroidery and Stenciled Blocks

45″ x 67″

Materials

▷ 4 yards of 45″-wide black watered silk for quilt top and backing

▷ 2 yards of 36″-wide bright red velveteen for mullions and border

▷ ½ old twin-size sheet for crazy block backing

▷ 2 yards of 45″-wide unbleached muslin for interlining

▷ An assortment of 10 old silk neckties, predominantly blues and reds for crazy blocks

▷ 4-6 skeins of 6-ply red embroidery floss

▷ 2 (5″ x 15″) sheets of frosted Mylar

▷ X-acto-type knife for cutting stencils

▷ Piece of glass for cutting base

▷ 1 (No. 4) stiff, round stencil brush

▷ Chromium oxide green acrylic paint

▷ White acrylic paint for mixing light green shade

▷ Cadmium red light acrylic paint

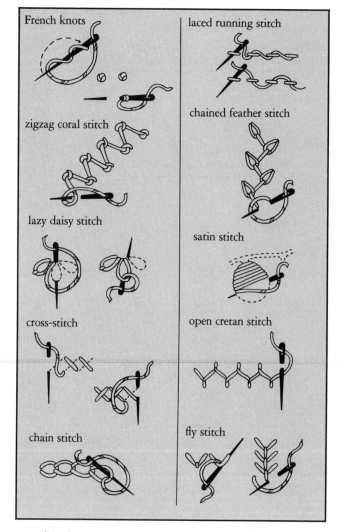

French knots · laced running stitch · zigzag coral stitch · chained feather stitch · lazy daisy stitch · satin stitch · cross-stitch · open cretan stitch · chain stitch · fly stitch

Cutting and Piecing

The unbleached muslin and old sheet must be washed and ironed. Trim selvage edges.

Cut fourteen 5½″ x 15½″ blocks from the black watered silk. The stenciled design will be painted on these blocks after the top is made.

Cut fourteen 7½″ x 17½″ blocks from the old sheet. These blocks will be the backing for the crazy blocks and will be trimmed to size later.

To make the crazy blocks, cut the silk neckties in random shapes. Press under the raw edges and pin to the blocks made from the old sheet. Topstitch by machine near the edges of the silk fabric.

Embellish the blocks with a variety of fancy embroidery stitches, using the red embroidery floss. Work the stitches to cover the machine stitching.

When the embroidery work is completed, trim each crazy quilt block to 5½″ x 15½″.

Cut twenty-four 1½″ x 15½″ strips and three 1½″ x 41½″ strips from the red velveteen for mullion strips around the crazy blocks and black blocks.

Piece six short mullion strips to the long sides of seven

blocks, alternating crazy blocks and black blocks to make a horizontal row. Repeat with remaining blocks, making three more rows. Two rows will start and end with crazy blocks, and two rows will start and end with black blocks. Piece the four rows together with the three long mullion strips. The addition of black squares at the corners of the blocks on the red mullion strips is optional.

Cut two 1½″ x 43½″ strips and two 1½″ x 63½″ strips from the red velveteen for a border. Stitch in place.

Place one sheet of Mylar on the American Beauty Rose pattern on the following page, and trace the red parts of the design. With the second sheet of Mylar, trace the green parts. Cut the stencils on the glass.

Paint the green leaves and stems first, mixing white with the green paint to make a lighter shade. Then

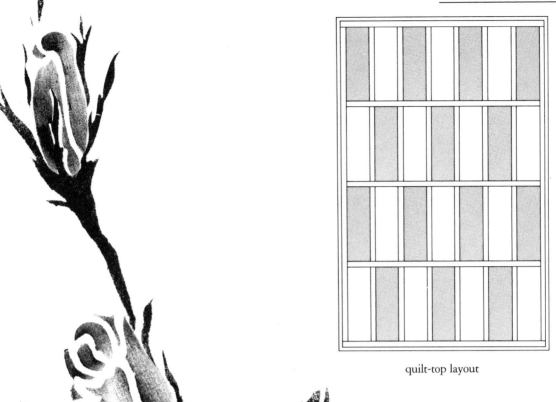

quilt-top layout

paint the red roses.

Allow the paint to dry overnight, and set with a hot, dry iron. Test the hot iron on a scrap of fabric first. Use a pressing cloth to avoid scorching.

Assembling and Finishing

Layer the backing, one thickness of unbleached muslin, and the quilt top. Baste together.

Quilt along all the seams over the entire quilt.

To finish the edges, do not trim the backing and inter-lining even with the quilt top. Leave an extra 1¼" on all sides of the backing and interlining for a border. Bring the backing and interlining to the quilt top. Fold under and pin. Hem to the edge of the red border on the quilt top. ♡

ROSE WREATH WITH TULIPS
(color plate 14)

Beginning

Patchwork Quilt with Stenciled Blocks

35½" x 51"

Materials

▷ 3 yards of 45"-wide unbleached muslin for quilt-top blocks and backing

▷ 1½ yards of 36"-wide bright blue cotton fabric for mullions and border

▷ ½ yard of 36"-wide dark green calico print for framing large blocks

▷ Quilt batting, crib size

▷ 1 (12"-square) sheet of frosted Mylar

▷ 1 (3" x 13") sheet of frosted Mylar

▷ X-acto-type knife for cutting stencils

▷ Piece of glass for cutting base

▷ 1 (No. 4) stiff, round stencil brush

▷ Hooker's green acrylic paint

▷ Cerulean blue acrylic paint, or any color that harmonizes with the blue calico

Cutting and Piecing

All fabric must be washed and ironed. Trim selvage edges.

Cut six 11½"-square blocks from the muslin.

Cut twelve 1½" x 11½" strips and twelve 1½" x 13½" strips of green calico to frame the unbleached muslin blocks.

Piece two short green strips to opposite sides of a muslin block. Piece two longer green strips to the other sides of the muslin block. Repeat for the five remaining blocks.

Cut four 3" x 13½" strips and one 3" x 44½" strip from the bright blue fabric to make mullion strips around the muslin blocks and green frames.

Piece two short blue strips to three large blocks, making a vertical row. Repeat for the three remaining large blocks. Piece the long blue strip to the two rows.

Cut two 5" x 38" strips and two 5" x 44½" strips from the blue fabric for a border. Stitch in place.

Place the square sheet of Mylar on the Rose Wreath pattern on the following page, and trace. On the second sheet of Mylar, trace the small border design outlining the large blocks (see page 133, top, in the Portfolio section). Cut the stencils on the glass.

Use masking tape to block out parts of the stencil that will be painted with different colors. To shade the blue flowers, paint the outer edges more heavily and let the fabric show through the inner parts.

Allow the paint to dry overnight, and set with a hot, dry iron. Use a pressing cloth to avoid scorching.

Assembling and Finishing

Mark the quilting design below (or a design of your choice) on the mullion strips, using a No. 3 (hard) lead pencil or dressmaker's marking pencil.

Layer the backing, batting, and top. Baste together.

Outline quilt all parts of the stenciled design. Quilt the penciled-in design on the mullion strips, and quilt along all seams.

To finish the edges, bring the backing material and batting to the front of the quilt. Turn under to make a 1" hem, and pin. Hem to the quilt top. ♡

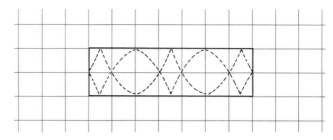

quilting design
1 square = 1 inch

TURKEY TRACKS
(color plate 15)

Intermediate

Whole-Cloth Quilt with Stenciled Design
60″ x 78″

Materials

▷ 4½ yards of 36″-wide unbleached muslin for quilt backing

▷ 1 twin-size light tan polyester/cotton–blend bed sheet for quilt top

▷ Quilt batting, twin size

▷ 2 (10″-square) sheets of frosted Mylar

▷ X-acto-type knife for cutting stencils

▷ Piece of glass for cutting base

▷ 1 (No. 4) stiff, round stencil brush

▷ Burnt umber acrylic paint

▷ Cadmium red light acrylic paint

Stenciling

All fabric must be washed and ironed. Trim selvage edges. Trim uneven edges, if any, from the top and bottom of the sheet. The top and bottom must be perfectly square to the sides.

Fold the tan fabric into quarters, and press folded edges with a warm iron. These creases will act as guidelines for positioning the stencils.

Using a yardstick and a No. 3 (hard) lead pencil or dressmaker's marking pencil, mark 9″ squares on the tan fabric, measuring from the pressed guidelines. Mark six squares across and eight squares

down. Mark a border line around the quilt top ½″ from the outer edges of the squares. All lines must be accurately marked. Remember, pencil lines are very hard to remove, so plan carefully before drawing.

Place one sheet of Mylar on the Turkey Track pattern on the following page, and trace just the burnt umber parts of the design (see the photo). Place the second piece of Mylar over the pattern, and trace the red section. Be sure to mark the top on the stencil sheets so the patterns will always match up the same way. Cut the stencils on the glass.

Paint all the burnt umber parts first, centering the design in the penciled squares. Then paint the second stencil, matching top to top. Remember that a stencil does not have to be painted solidly. By applying paint unevenly, you'll give the stencil a textured effect and add interest.

Allow the paint to dry overnight, and set with a hot, dry iron. Use a pressing cloth to avoid scorching.

Assembling and Finishing

Layer the backing, batting, and quilt top. Baste all three layers together.

Outline quilt all parts of the stenciled design. Quilt all penciled-in lines — they will simulate pieced blocks.

To finish the edges, bring the quilt-top fabric and batting to the back side, turn under to make a 1″ hem, and pin. Hem to the quilt backing.   ♡

SONG BIRDS

(color plate 16)

Beginning

Patchwork Quilt with Stenciled Blocks

33″ x 47″

Materials

▷ 3 yards of 36″-wide unbleached muslin for quilt-top blocks and backing

▷ 1½ yards of 36″-wide light tan cotton fabric for mullions and border

▷ Quilt batting, crib size

▷ 1 (12″-square) sheet of frosted Mylar

▷ X-acto-type knife for cutting stencils

▷ Piece of glass for cutting base

▷ Leather or paper punch

▷ 1 (No. 4) stiff, round stencil brush

▷ Burnt sienna acrylic paint

▷ Burnt umber acrylic paint

▷ Yellow oxide acrylic paint

Cutting and Piecing

All fabric must be washed and ironed. Trim selvage edges.

Cut six 11½″-square blocks from the muslin.

Cut four 3½″ x 11½″ strips and one 3½″ x 39½″ strip from the tan fabric to form mullions around the muslin blocks. Piece two short tan mullion strips to three large unbleached muslin blocks, making a horizontal row. Repeat with the second row. Piece the long strip to the two rows of blocks.

Cut two 5½″ x 25½″ strips and two 5½″ x 49½″ strips from the tan fabric for a border. Piece the short strips to the sides and the long strips to the top and bottom of the quilt.

Place the Mylar on the bird pattern on the following page and trace only the body of the bird and the leaf designs. In the corner of the Mylar sheet, trace the bird's tail and wing. Cut the stencils on the glass.

The berry holes in the stencil can be punched with a leather or paper punch, or they can be cut by hand.

Paint the body of the bird with yellow oxide paint. Paint the tail and wing with burnt umber. Paint the leaves with burnt sienna, using masking tape to cover the berries. Move the tape, and paint the berries with burnt umber.

Allow the paint to dry overnight, and set with a hot, dry iron. Use a pressing cloth to avoid scorching.

Assembling and Finishing

Mark the quilting design below on the mullion strips and borders with a No. 3 (hard) lead pencil or dressmaker's marking pencil.

Layer the backing, batting, and top. Baste together.

Quilt ⅜″ from the seams inside the muslin blocks. Outline quilt the stenciled leaves and stem lines. Quilt the penciled-in design lines on the mullion strips and border.

To finish the edges, bring the backing and batting to the front side, turn under and pin, making a 1″ muslin border. Hem to the quilt top.

Hanging loops (2″ x 5″) can be made from the light tan fabric and added to the top of the quilt to hold a wooden rod. ♡

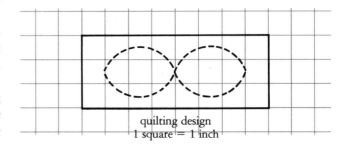

quilting design
1 square = 1 inch

ROSE OF SHARON

(color plate 17)

Patchwork Quilt with Stenciled Blocks

39½″ x 53″

Materials

▷ 3 yards of 42″-wide unbleached muslin for quilt-top blocks, border, and backing

▷ 2 yards of 36″-wide light green cotton fabric for mullions and border

▷ Quilt batting, crib size

▷ 2 (12″-square) sheets of frosted Mylar

▷ X-acto-type knife for cutting stencils

▷ Piece of glass for cutting base

▷ 1 (No. 4) stiff, round stencil brush

▷ Hooker's green acrylic paint

▷ Cerulean blue acrylic paint

Cutting and Piecing

All fabric must be washed and ironed. Trim selvage edges.

Cut six 11½″-square blocks from the unbleached muslin.

Cut eight 3″ x 11½″ strips and three 3″ x 43½″ strips from the light green fabric to form mullion strips around the unbleached muslin blocks.

Piece four short mullion strips to three muslin blocks, making a vertical row. Repeat with remaining short mullion strips and blocks. Piece the three long mullion strips to the two rows.

Cut two 3″ x 35″ strips and two 3″ x 43½″ strips from the muslin for a border. Stitch in place.

Cut two 4″ x 35″ strips and two 4″ x 55½″ strips from the light green fabric for the second border. Stitch in place. Press all seams onto the light green fabric.

Place one sheet of Mylar on the Rose of Sharon pattern on the following page, and trace just the green parts of the pattern (see the photo). Place the second sheet of Mylar on the pattern, and trace just the blue parts. Mark the top on both stencils. Cut the stencils on the glass.

Paint the green parts first. When painting the blue parts, be sure to align the stencil tops.

Allow the paint to dry overnight, and set with a hot, dry iron. Use a pressing cloth to avoid scorching.

quilt-top layout

Assembling and Finishing

Layer the backing, batting, and top. Baste together.

Quilt ⅜″ from both sides of all seams. Outline quilt all parts of the stenciled design. If you hold the quilting lines close to the painted flowers, they will puff up and create an effect of trapunto work.

To finish the edges, bring the backing and batting to the front side, fold under to make a 1″ hem, and pin. Hem to the quilt top.

♡

CIRCLE OF TULIPS
(color plate 18)

Patchwork Quilt with Stenciled Blocks
47″ x 61″

Materials

▷ 5 yards of 36″-wide unbleached muslin for quilt-top blocks, border, and backing

▷ 2 yards of 36″-wide dark green dotted cotton fabric for mullions and border

▷ 1½ yards of 36″-wide bright red cotton fabric for border

▷ Quilt batting, twin size

▷ 1 (12″-square) sheet of frosted Mylar

▷ 1 (4″ x 8″) sheet of frosted Mylar

▷ X-acto-type knife for cutting stencils

▷ Piece of glass for cutting base

▷ 1 (No. 4) stiff, round stencil brush

▷ Hooker's green acrylic paint

▷ Cadmium red medium acrylic paint, or any color that harmonizes with the red fabric

Cutting and Piecing

All fabric must be washed and ironed. Trim selvage edges.

Cut six 11½″-square blocks from the muslin.

Cut four 3½″ x 11½″ strips and three 3½″ x 39½″ strips of dark green fabric to form mullion strips around the six muslin blocks.

Piece four short mullion strips to three muslin blocks, making a vertical row. Repeat with remaining short mullion strips and blocks. Piece the three long mullion strips to the two rows.

Cut two 3½″ x 31½″ strips from the dark green fabric for a top and bottom border. Stitch in place.

Cut two 2½″ x 35½″ strips and two 2½″ x 45½″ strips from the red fabric for a border around the mullion strips. Stitch in place.

Cut two 4″ x 42½″ strips and two 4″ x 49½″ strips from the muslin fabric to form a second border. Stitch in place.

Cut two 4″ x 49½″ strips and two 4″ x 56½″ strips from

the dark green fabric for the outer border. Stitch in place. Press all seams onto the green or red fabric.

Place the 12″-square sheet of Mylar on the Circle of Tulips pattern on the following page, and trace. Place the second sheet of Mylar on the border design (see page 132, left, in the Portfolio section), and trace. Cut the stencils on the glass.

Paint the green areas of the tulip stencil first (see the photo). Then paint the red areas. Use masking tape to block out parts of the stencil that will be painted with different colors.

Paint the border. Use one of the hearts in the center of the tulip pattern to stencil the red hearts in the border.

Allow the paint to dry overnight, and set with a hot, dry iron. Use a pressing cloth to avoid scorching.

Assembling and Finishing

Use a No. 3 (hard) lead pencil or dressmaker's marking pencil to mark a circle around each of the stenciled tulip designs (an 11″ dinner plate works well for this). Mark a 4″ circle around each group of four hearts in the center of the stenciled designs. Mark the quilting design below on the green mullion strips. Use the border stencil of the leaves for a quilting design on the outer muslin border.

Layer the backing, batting, and top. Baste together.

Quilt the penciled-in circles and design lines. Quilt all parts of the stenciled design, and quilt along the seams.

To finish the edges, bring the backing and batting to the front side. Turn under to make a 1″ hem, and pin to the dark green fabric. Hem to the quilt top. ♡

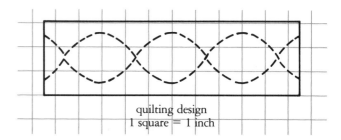

quilting design
1 square = 1 inch

HEARTS AND FLOWERS
(color plate 19)

Intermediate

Patchwork Quilt with Stenciled Blocks
57″ x 66″

Materials

▷ 5½ yards of 36″-wide unbleached muslin for quilt-top blocks and backing

▷ 2 yards of 36″-wide medium-green small calico print for quilt-top blocks and border

▷ 2 yards of 36″-wide black cotton fabric for quilt borders

▷ Quilt batting, twin size

▷ 1 (10″-square) sheet of frosted Mylar

▷ X-acto-type knife for cutting stencils

▷ Piece of glass for cutting base

▷ 1 (No. 4) stiff, round stencil brush

▷ Black acrylic paint

Cutting and Piecing

All fabric must be washed and ironed. Trim selvage edges.

Cut fifteen 9½″-square blocks from the unbleached muslin.

Cut fifteen 9½″-square blocks from the green calico print.

Piece the 9½″ blocks together, alternating the colors in a checkerboard pattern, as shown in the layout. Piece five blocks across and six blocks down.

Cut two 3″ x 45½″ strips and two 3″ x 59½″ strips from the black fabric to border the blocks. Stitch in place.

Cut two 3″ x 50½″ strips and two 3″ x 64½″ strips from the green calico to make a second border. Stitch in place.

Cut two 2½″ x 55½″ strips and two 2½″ x 68½″ strips from the black fabric for the outer border. Stitch in place.

Place the Mylar on the Hearts and Flowers pattern on the following page, and trace. Cut the stencil on the glass.

Stencil paint all 30 blocks, centering the stencil on each.

Allow the paint to dry overnight, and set with a hot, dry iron. Use a pressing cloth to avoid scorching.

quilt-top layout

Assembling and Finishing

Layer the backing, batting, and top. Baste together.

Outline quilt every part of the stenciled design. Quilt ⅜″ from the seams in all blocks and along the borders.

To finish the edges, bring the top fabric and batting to the quilt back. Fold under to make a 1″ hem, and pin. Hem to the backing. ♡

CREEPING PERIWINKLE
(cover and color plate 20)

Patchwork Quilt with Stenciled Strips

67″ x 72″

Materials

▷ 2 twin-size white polyester/cotton–blend bed sheets for quilt-top strips, border, and backing

▷ 2 yards of 45″-wide (or more) tan-and-rose striped calico print for quilt-top strips

▷ Quilt batting, twin size

▷ 1 (5″ x 17″) sheet of frosted Mylar

▷ X-acto-type knife for cutting stencils

▷ Piece of glass for cutting base

▷ 1 (No. 4) stiff, round stencil brush

▷ Burnt umber acrylic paint, or any color that harmonizes with calico print

Cutting and Piecing

All fabric must be washed and ironed. Trim selvage edges.

Cut eleven 3½″ x 68½″ strips from the striped calico print. (The width may vary depending upon the stripe pattern of the fabric. Adjust the width of the white strips to match that of the calico strips.) The cutting line should follow the stripe in the fabric.

Cut twelve 3½″ x 68½″ strips from the white fabric.

Piece all strips together, alternating colors and ending with a white strip on either side.

Cut two 3½″ x 69½″ strips from the white fabric for top and bottom borders of the quilt. Stitch in place.

Place the Mylar on the Creeping Periwinkle patterns on the following page, and trace the two patterns end to end. Trace the small pattern above the large one, adjusting the spacing between the two to match the rest of the pattern. Refer to the photo for the movement of the stem line. With the two patterns, the stencil has a 15″ repeat. Cut the stencil on the glass.

Starting at the top of the quilt and working down each white strip, paint the stencil with burnt umber paint. When repeating the pattern, keep the spacing consistent each time.

Allow the paint to dry overnight, and set with a hot, dry iron. Use a pressing cloth to avoid scorching.

Assembling and Finishing

Mark small circles around each stenciled flower with a No. 3 (hard) lead pencil or dressmaker's marking pencil.

Layer the backing, batting, and top. Baste together.

Quilt along all seams. Quilt the penciled-in circles around the stenciled flowers, and quilt along the stem lines.

To finish the edges, turn the quilt top and batting to the back side. Fold under to make a 1″ hem, and pin. Hem to the backing. ♡

ART NOUVEAU
(color plate 21)

Advanced

Whole-Cloth Quilt with Stenciled Design
63″ x 76″

Materials

▷ 1 twin-size light tan polyester/cotton–blend bed sheet for quilt top

▷ 1 twin-size white polyester/cotton–blend bed sheet for quilt backing

▷ Quilt batting, twin size

▷ 4 skeins of 6-ply light tan embroidery floss

▷ Newspaper or brown kraft paper

▷ 1 (24″ x 38″) sheet of frosted Mylar

▷ 2 (5″ x 12″) sheets of frosted Mylar

▷ X-acto-type knife for cutting stencils

▷ Piece of glass for cutting base

▷ 1 (No. 4) stiff, round stencil brush

▷ Cerulean blue acrylic paint for the flowers

▷ Burnt umber acrylic paint for shading the hair

▷ Payne's gray acrylic paint for the border designs

Stenciling

All fabric must be washed and ironed. Trim selvage edges. Trim uneven edges, if any, from the top and bottom of each sheet. The top and bottom must be perfectly square to the sides.

Tape several large sheets of newspaper together or use brown kraft paper and make a large oval 35″ across and 49″ long. Put aside to be used later.

Using the two 5″ x 12″ sheets of Mylar, trace each of the Art Nouveau border patterns (page 130 in the Portfolio section) on a sheet of Mylar. Cut the stencils on the glass.

Mark 1″ grid lines on the frosted side of the large Mylar sheet for the stencil of the girl. Enlarge the head of the girl (from the diagram on the following page) on the Mylar. Cut the stencil on the glass.

Plan the layout of the stencil design (see the photo). Fold the quilt-top fabric in quarters, and press the folded edges with a warm iron. These crease lines will act as guidelines for centering the stencils and marking the large oval. The crease lines must be accurate.

Spread out the quilt top on a large, flat surface (such as a Ping-Pong table). Center the newspaper oval in the middle of the quilt top and tape it down with masking tape. Using a No. 3 (hard) lead pencil or dressmaker's marking pencil, draw a line around the oval pattern. Measure a second line 4½″ outside of the oval, making many little pencil dots as you measure. After you've worked all the way around the oval, connect the dots with a line, forming a border.

Make a border around the edge of the quilt: Measure 3½″ in from the edge, and pencil a line all around the quilt. Measure 3″ in from the first line, and pencil a second line around the quilt. The quilt-top material must be absolutely square for your quilt to be perfect.

With the pencil work finished, proceed with the stencil painting. Center the large stencil inside the oval, hold in place with masking tape, and paint the design. Remember that a good stencil does not have to be painted solidly. Before painting, experiment on fabric scraps with different techniques such as stippling and streaking the brush over the fabric. Accent lines may be added with a black laundry marker after painting.

Plan the stenciled border around the large oval. Work the design from the four crease lines and make the design units evenly spaced. Spend time to make the layout correct. Paint the border design with Payne's gray paint.

Plan the outer border of the quilt in much the same way. Start the design at the crease lines. When it is all worked out, paint with Payne's gray.

Allow the paint to dry overnight, and set with a hot, dry iron. Use a pressing cloth to avoid scorching.

Assembling and Finishing

Mark the entire background area around the oval with pencil dots 2″ apart, across and down. This entire area will be tied off with embroidery floss.

Layer the backing, batting, and top. Baste together.

Outline quilt all parts of the large stencil. Quilt the penciled-in lines for the oval border. Quilt the penciled-in lines for the outer border.

Using embroidery floss, tie off each pencil dot on the background.

To finish the edges, bring the quilt-top fabric and batting to the back side. Fold under to make a 1″ hem, and pin. Hem to the backing. ♡

1 square = 1 inch

BLUE WHIG ROSE

(color plate 22)

Intermediate

Patchwork Quilt with Stenciled Blocks

68½" x 83"

Materials

▷ 2 twin-size white polyester/cotton–blend bed sheets for quilt-top blocks, border, and backing

▷ 1 twin-size light blue polyester/cotton–blend bed sheet for mullions and borders

▷ Quilt batting, full size

▷ 1 (3" x 12") strip of frosted Mylar

▷ 1 (10"-square) sheet of frosted Mylar

▷ X-acto-type knife for cutting stencils

▷ Piece of glass for cutting base

▷ 1 (No. 4) stiff, round stencil brush

▷ Hooker's green acrylic paint

▷ Cerulean blue acrylic paint, or any blue that harmonizes with the blue fabric

Cutting and Piecing

All fabric must be washed and ironed. Trim selvage edges.

Cut twenty 10½"-square blocks from the white fabric.

Cut sixteen 5" x 10½" strips and five 5" x 68½" strips from the light blue sheet to form mullion strips around the white blocks.

Piece four short mullion strips to five white blocks, making a vertical row. Repeat with remaining white blocks, making three more rows. Piece the five long mullion strips to the four rows of blocks.

Cut two 5" x 63" strips from the light blue sheet to form top and bottom borders. Stitch in place.

Cut two 2½" x 67" strips and two 2½" x 77½" strips from the white sheet to form a border around the blue mullion strips. Stitch in place.

Cut two 2½" x 71" strips and two 2½" x 81½" strips from the light blue sheet for a final border. Stitch in place. Press seams onto the blue fabric.

Place the 10"-square sheet of Mylar on the Whig Rose pattern on the following page, and trace. Trace the small border design (see page 134, top or bottom, in the Portfolio section) on the 3" x 12" strip of Mylar. Cut the stencils on the glass.

Referring to the color plate, paint the Hooker's green parts first. Block out the blue parts of the stencil with masking tape. Paint the white blocks first, then paint the center design of the large stencil pattern on the corners of the mullion strips. Paint the green border around the large blocks. When painting the blue flowers, add a little texture by stippling the paint.

Allow the paint to dry overnight, and set with a hot, dry iron. Use a pressing cloth to avoid scorching.

Assembling and Finishing

Mark the quilting design below (or a design of your choice) on the wide blue mullion strips, using a No. 3 (hard) lead pencil or dressmaker's marking pencil. Using a large glass, draw a 3½" circle around each of the stenciled designs on the corners of the mullion strips.

Layer the backing, batting, and top. Baste together.

Outline quilt all parts of the stenciled design on the white blocks. Do not quilt the small border design around the blocks. Quilt along all seams, and quilt the penciled-in design lines on the mullion strips.

To finish the edges, bring the quilt-top fabric and batting to the back side. Fold under to make a 1" hem, and pin. Hem to the backing.   ♡

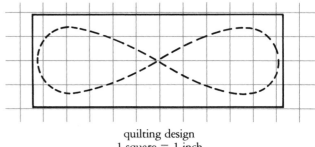

quilting design
1 square = 1 inch

DUTCH TULIPS
(color plate 23)

Patchwork Quilt with Stenciled Blocks
53½" x 74½"

Materials

▷ 6 yards of 36"-wide unbleached muslin for quilt-top blocks, border, and backing

▷ 3 yards of 36"-wide deep aqua cotton fabric for quilt-top blocks, framing strips, and border

▷ Quilt batting, twin size

▷ ¼ (3½ oz.) skein of 4-ply aqua wool yarn

▷ 1 (10"-square) sheet of frosted Mylar

▷ X-acto-type knife for cutting stencils

▷ Piece of glass for cutting base

▷ 1 (No. 4) stiff, round stencil brush

▷ 1 (9½"-square) piece of cardboard

▷ Aqua acrylic paint

▷ Burnt sienna acrylic paint

▷ Yellow oxide acrylic paint

Cutting and Piecing

All fabric must be washed and ironed. Trim selvage edges.

Cut six 12"-square blocks from the unbleached muslin.

Cut twelve 1½" x 12" strips and twelve 1½" x 14" strips from the aqua fabric to frame each of the muslin blocks. Piece two short and two long aqua strips to each of the muslin blocks. The rest of the quilt top is made of 9 nine-patch blocks.

Cut forty-three 5"-square blocks of unbleached muslin.

Cut thirty-eight 5"-square blocks of aqua fabric.

Make seven nine-patch blocks by piecing five unbleached muslin squares and four aqua squares, alternating squares in a checkerboard fashion (see the photo).

Make two nine-patch blocks by piecing four muslin squares and five aqua squares, alternating squares in a checkerboard fashion.

Assemble the quilt top by piecing the large muslin blocks and the nine-patch blocks as shown in the photo.

Cut two 2" x 50" strips and two 5" x 68" strips from the unbleached muslin for a border. Piece the 5"-wide strips to the sides. Piece the 2"-wide strips to the top and bottom.

Cut two 3½" x 56" strips and two 3½" x 71" strips of the aqua fabric to frame the unbleached muslin border. Stitch in place.

Place the Mylar on the Dutch Tulip pattern on the following page, and trace. Cut the stencil on the glass.

Paint the large tulips with aqua paint, the smaller flowers with burnt sienna, and the outer tips of the small flowers with yellow oxide. Use masking tape to cover parts of the stencil that will be painted with different colors.

Allow the paint to dry overnight, and set with a hot, dry iron. Use a pressing cloth to avoid scorching.

Assembling and Finishing

Using a large glass, draw a 3" circle in the center of each small unbleached muslin square. Draw 3" circles on the muslin borders on the sides of the quilt. Be sure to use a No. 3 (hard) lead pencil or dressmaker's marking pencil.

Make a 9½"-square cardboard template and round off the corners. Use the template to mark the quilting lines on the large stenciled blocks.

Layer the backing, batting, and top. Baste together.

Quilt all parts of the stenciled design in the large blocks. Quilt along all seams, and quilt all penciled-in lines.

Using the aqua yarn, add 1" ties in the center of each square of the nine-patch blocks and in the quilted circles on the border.

To finish the edges, bring the backing material and batting to the front side of the quilt. Fold under to make a 1" hem, and pin. Hem to the aqua border on the quilt top. ♡

HEARTS AND MORE HEARTS

(color plate 24)

Intermediate

Patchwork Quilt with Stenciled Blocks

47″ x 65″

Materials

▷ 6 yards of 36″-wide unbleached muslin for quilt-top blocks and backing

▷ 2 yards of 36″-wide light pink calico print for quilt-top blocks

▷ High-loft quilt batting, twin size

▷ ¼ (3½ oz.) skein of 4-ply off-white wool yarn

▷ 1 (10″-square) sheet of frosted Mylar

▷ 1 (4″-square) sheet of frosted Mylar

▷ X-acto-type knife for cutting stencils

▷ Piece of glass for cutting base

▷ 1 (No. 4) stiff, round stencil brush

▷ Cobalt blue acrylic paint

Cutting and Piecing

All fabric must be washed and ironed. Trim selvage edges.

This quilt is made of 18 nine-patch blocks and 17 octagon blocks. Each nine-patch block will have five unbleached muslin squares and four pink calico squares.

To make the 18 nine-patch blocks, cut ninety 3½″ squares from the unbleached muslin and seventy-two 3½″ squares from the pink calico.

Piece the nine-patch blocks first, alternating the patches in each block as shown in the layout.

For the octagon blocks, cut seventeen 9½″ squares from the unbleached muslin and sixty-eight 3½″ squares from the pink calico.

To make an octagon block, pin (with right sides together) a pink calico square to each corner of a muslin square. Even up the pink squares with the corners of the muslin square. Stitch diagonally through the pink square. Trim off the excess corners and press the seams onto the pink fabric. Repeat for all octagon blocks.

To assemble the quilt top, alternate the nine-patch blocks with the octagon blocks in a checkerboard fashion. Piece five blocks across and seven blocks down, placing a nine-patch block in each corner.

Place the 10″-square sheet of Mylar on the large heart pattern on the following page, and trace. Trace the small heart pattern on the 4″-square sheet of Mylar. Cut the stencils on the glass.

Paint only the unbleached muslin blocks. Paint the large heart pattern on the large blocks first, and then paint the small heart pattern on the nine-patch blocks.

Allow the paint to dry overnight, and set with a hot, dry iron. Use a pressing cloth to avoid scorching.

quilt-top layout

Assembling and Finishing

Layer the backing, batting, and top. Baste together.

Because of the high-loft batting, there is no need for quilting.

Using the off-white yarn, tie off the quilt in the center of each of the large and small unbleached muslin blocks. Add a tie to the center of each of the four sides of the large unbleached muslin blocks.

To finish the edges, do not trim the backing and batting even with the quilt top. Leave an extra 1¼″ on all sides of the backing and batting for a border. Bring the backing and batting to the front side of the quilt. Turn under to make a 1″ hem, and pin. Hem to the edge of the quilt top. ♡

ROSE WREATH AND BUD

(cover and color plate 25)

Patchwork Quilt with Stenciled Blocks
38½″ x 52″

Materials

▷ 3 yards of 42″-wide unbleached muslin for the quilt-top blocks, border, and backing

▷ 1½ yards of 36″-wide dark green cotton fabric for mullions and border

▷ Quilt batting, crib size

▷ 2 (12″-square) sheets of frosted Mylar

▷ X-acto-type knife for cutting stencils

▷ Piece of glass for cutting base

▷ 1 (No. 4) stiff, round stencil brush

▷ Hooker's green acrylic paint

▷ Cadmium red medium acrylic paint

▷ White acrylic paint for mixing with the red paint to make pink

Cutting and Piecing

All fabric must be washed and ironed. Trim selvage edges.

Cut six 11½″-square blocks from the muslin.

Cut eight 3″ x 11½″ strips and three 3″ x 43½″ strips from the dark green fabric to form mullion strips around the six muslin blocks.

Piece four short mullion strips to three muslin blocks, making a vertical row. Repeat with three remaining muslin blocks. Piece the three long mullion strips to the two rows of muslin blocks.

Cut two 3″ x 35″ strips and two 3″ x 43½″ strips from the unbleached muslin fabric for a border around the mullion strips. Stitch in place.

Cut two 3″ x 41″ strips and two 3″ x 48½″ strips from the dark green fabric to form a second border. Stitch in place. Press all seams onto the dark green fabric.

Place the Mylar on the Rose Wreath pattern on the following page, and trace just the green areas of the design (see the photo). Using the second sheet of Mylar, trace just the pink areas. Mark the top on both stencils. Cut the stencils on the glass.

Paint the green areas first. When painting the pink areas, be sure to line up the tops of the stencils.

Allow the paint to dry overnight, and set with a hot, dry iron. Use a pressing cloth to avoid scorching.

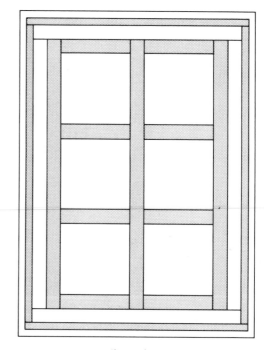

quilt-top layout

Assembling and Finishing

Layer the backing, batting, and top. Baste together.

Quilt ⅜″ from the seams on all blocks and borders. Outline quilt all parts of the stenciled design. Hold the quilting lines close to the painted flowers to make them puff up and create the effect of trapunto work.

To finish the edges, bring the backing material and batting to the front of the quilt. Fold under to make a 1″ hem, and pin to the dark green fabric. Hem to the quilt top. ♡

CHRISTMAS ROSE OF SHARON
(color plate 26)

Beginning

Patchwork Quilt with Stenciled Blocks

43" x 57"

Materials

▷ 3 yards of 45"-wide unbleached muslin for quilt-top blocks and backing

▷ 2 yards of 36"-wide bright red dotted cotton fabric for mullions and border

▷ 1½ yards of 36"-wide light green cotton fabric for border

▷ Quilt batting, crib size

▷ 2 (12"-square) sheets of frosted Mylar

▷ 1 (6" x 12") sheet of frosted Mylar (for optional border stencils)

▷ X-acto-type knife for cutting stencils

▷ Piece of glass for cutting base

▷ 1 (No. 4) stiff, round stencil brush

▷ Hooker's green acrylic paint

▷ Vivid lime green acrylic paint

▷ Cadmium red medium acrylic paint, or any color that harmonizes with red dotted fabric

Cutting and Piecing

All fabric must be washed and ironed. Trim selvage edges.

Cut six 11½"-square blocks from the muslin.

Cut eight 3½" x 11½" strips and three 3½" x 45½" strips from the red dotted fabric to form mullion strips around the muslin blocks.

Piece four short mullion strips to three muslin blocks, making a vertical row. Repeat with the three remaining muslin blocks. Piece the three long mullion strips to the two rows of muslin blocks.

Cut two 2½" x 31½" strips and two 2½" x 49½" strips from the light green fabric to make a border around the mullion strips. Stitch in place.

Cut two 5½" x 35½" strips and two 5½" x 59½" strips from the red dotted fabric to make a final border. Stitch in place. Press all seams onto the red dotted fabric.

Place one sheet of Mylar on the Rose of Sharon pattern on page 83, and trace just the green areas (see the

photo). Using the second sheet of Mylar, trace just the red areas. Mark the top of both stencils. The border stencils on the following page are optional. Cut the stencils on the glass.

Paint the dark Hooker's green first, then the vivid lime green for the leaves, and last, the cadmium red (refer to the photo). To shade the flowers, paint the outer edges more heavily and let the fabric show through the inner parts. Paint the borders with Hooker's green.

Allow the paint to dry overnight, and set with a hot, dry iron. Use a pressing cloth to avoid scorching.

Assembling and Finishing

Layer the backing, batting, and top. Baste together.

Outline quilt all parts of the stenciled design. Quilt ⅜" away from all seams on the blocks and on the red mullion strips and borders.

To finish the edges, bring the backing fabric and batting to the front of the quilt. Fold under to make a 1" hem, and pin. Hem to the quilt top.   ♡

Rose of Sharon pattern (use full-size pattern on page 83)

OAK LEAF AND REEL
(color plate 27)

Patchwork Quilt with Stenciled Blocks
44″ x 58″

Materials

▷ 1 twin-size white polyester/cotton–blend bed sheet for quilt-top blocks, border, and backing

▷ 2 yards of 36″-wide pale yellow fabric for mullions and border

▷ Quilt batting, twin size

▷ 1 (10″-square) sheet of frosted Mylar

▷ 1 (4″ x 12″) sheet of frosted Mylar

▷ X-acto-type knife for cutting stencils

▷ Piece of glass for cutting base

▷ 1 (No. 4) stiff, round stencil brush

▷ Burnt umber acrylic paint

▷ Yellow oxide acrylic paint

▷ Chromium oxide green acrylic paint

Cutting and Piecing

All fabric must be washed and ironed. Trim selvage edges.

Cut six 10½″-square blocks from the white fabric.

Cut four 4½″ x 10½″ strips and three 4½″ x 38½″ strips from the yellow fabric for mullion strips around the white blocks.

Piece two short mullion strips to three white blocks, making a vertical row. Repeat with the three remaining white blocks. Piece the three long mullion strips to the two rows.

Cut two 4½″ x 32½″ strips from the yellow fabric for the top and bottom borders. Stitch in place.

Cut two 4½″ x 40½″ strips and two 4½″ x 46½″ strips from the white sheet to form a border around the mullion strips. Stitch in place.

Cut two 4½″ x 48½″ strips and two 4½″ x 54½″ strips from the yellow fabric to form the final border. Stitch in place. Press all seams onto the yellow fabric.

Place the 10″-square sheet of Mylar on the Oak Leaf and Reel pattern on the following page, and trace. Trace the border design (see page 132, left, in the Portfolio section) on the second sheet of Mylar. Cut the stencils on the glass.

Use masking tape to block out parts of the stencil that will be painted with different colors. When painting the large areas, create a textured feeling by stippling the paint.

Plan the layout of the pattern for the border design, and paint the border.

Allow the paint to dry overnight, and set with a hot, dry iron. Use a pressing cloth to avoid scorching.

Assembling and Finishing

Layer the backing, batting, and top. Baste together.

Outline quilt all parts of the stenciled design on the large blocks and all parts of the border stencil. Quilt ⅝″ from all seams on the blocks, mullion strips, and borders.

To finish the edges, bring half of the yellow border and the batting to the back of the quilt. Fold under to form a 1″ hem, and pin. Hem to the backing. ♡

ART DECO
(color plate 28)

Whole-Cloth Quilt with Stenciled Design
62″ x 78½″

Materials

▷ 1 twin-size dark blue polyester/cotton–blend bed sheet for quilt top

▷ 1 twin-size white polyester/cotton–blend bed sheet for quilt backing

▷ Quilt batting, twin size

▷ White lead pencil

▷ 2 (18″ x 24″) sheets of frosted Mylar (large, lightweight cardboard boxes, poster board, or tagboard can be substituted)

▷ X-acto-type knife for cutting stencils

▷ Piece of glass for cutting base

▷ 1 (No. 4) stiff, round stencil brush

▷ Vivid lime green acrylic paint

▷ Light violet acrylic paint

▷ Yellow oxide acrylic paint

Stenciling

All fabric must be washed and ironed. Trim selvage edges. Trim uneven edges, if any, from top and bottom of each sheet. The top and bottom must be perfectly square to the sides.

Fold the top dark blue fabric into quarters. Press folded edges with a warm iron. These creases will act as guidelines for positioning the stencils.

With a white lead pencil and ruler, mark a line 2½″ from the edge around the entire quilt top. This line will be the cutoff point for the stencil pattern and will create a border effect.

With a regular lead pencil, mark 1″ grid lines on the frosted side of the Mylar sheets. Enlarge the cattail and cattail/dragonfly patterns (from the diagrams on the following page) on the Mylar, using a separate sheet for each pattern. Cut the stencils on the glass.

Plan the layout of the stencil design (see the photo). Using the white lead pencil, make dots on the fabric to mark the positions of the patterns. Tape the stencils to the fabric when painting.

Use masking tape to cover the sections of the stencils that will be painted with different colors. Change taped areas when changing colors.

Since the dark blue fabric will absorb the paint, make sure the painted areas have sufficient paint to show the pattern before removing the stencil.

Allow the paint to dry overnight, and set with a hot, dry iron. Use a pressing cloth to avoid scorching.

Assembling and Finishing

Layer the backing, batting, and top. Baste together.

Outline quilt all parts of the stenciled design. Quilt the penciled-in border lines.

To finish the edges, turn the top fabric and batting to the back side, fold under, and pin. Hem to backing, following the quilted border line.   ♡

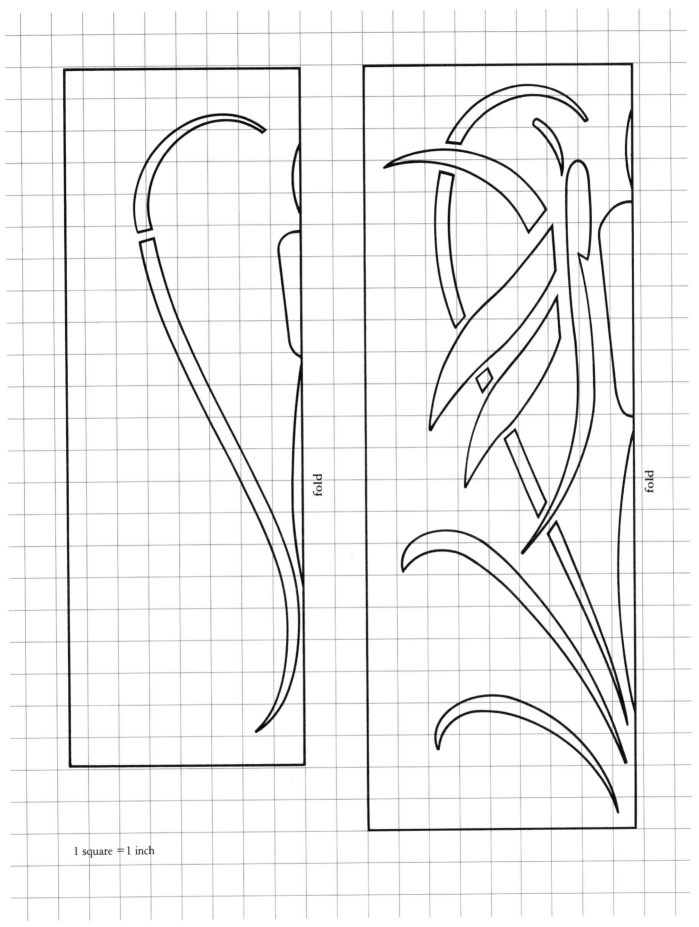

fold

fold

1 square = 1 inch

LAUREL LEAF
(color plate 29)

Patchwork Quilt with Stenciled Blocks

45″ x 59″

Materials

▷ 3 yards of 45″-wide unbleached muslin for quilt-top blocks, border, and backing

▷ 2 yards of 36″-wide tan calico print for mullions and border

▷ Quilt batting, twin size

▷ 1 (11″-square) sheet of frosted Mylar

▷ X-acto-type knife for cutting stencils

▷ Piece of glass for cutting base

▷ 1 (No. 4) stiff, round stencil brush

▷ Burnt sienna acrylic paint, or any color that harmonizes with calico print

Cutting and Piecing

All fabric must be washed and ironed. Trim selvage edges.

Cut six 11½″-square blocks from the muslin.

Cut eight 3½″ x 11½″ strips and three 3½″ x 45½″ strips from the tan fabric to form mullion strips around the muslin blocks.

Piece four short mullion strips with three muslin blocks, making a vertical row. Repeat with the three remaining muslin blocks. Piece the three long mullion strips to the two rows.

Cut two 3½″ x 37½″ strips and two 3½″ x 45½″ strips from the unbleached muslin to form a border around the mullion strips. Stitch in place.

Cut two 5½″ x 49½″ strips and two 5½″ x 51½″ strips

from the tan fabric for the outer border. Stitch in place.

Place the Mylar on the Laurel Leaf pattern on the following page, and trace. Cut the stencil on the glass.

Paint all large unbleached muslin blocks.

Allow the paint to dry overnight, and set with a hot, dry iron. Use a pressing cloth to avoid scorching.

Assembling and Finishing

Using a No. 3 (hard) lead pencil or dressmaker's marking pencil, mark the quilting design below (or a design of your choice) on the mullion strips and borders. Refer to the photo for proper placement of the design.

Layer the backing, batting, and top. Baste together.

Outline quilt all parts of the stenciled design. Quilt the penciled-in lines on the mullions and borders.

To finish the edges, bring the backing fabric and batting to the front side of the quilt. Fold under to make a 1″ hem, and pin. Hem to the quilt top. ♡

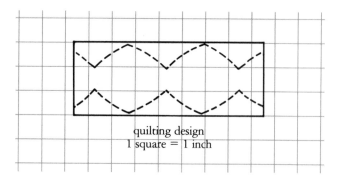

quilting design
1 square = 1 inch

PETER RABBIT
(color plate 30)

Patchwork Quilt with Stenciled Blocks
52″ x 61″

Materials

▷ 1 twin-size light tan outing-flannel bed sheet for quilt-top blocks and backing

▷ 2 yards of 36″-wide green-and-tan plaid outing flannel for quilt-top blocks and border

▷ Quilt batting, twin size

▷ ¼ (3½ oz.) skein of 4-ply tan wool yarn

▷ 3 (5″-square) sheets of frosted Mylar

▷ X-acto-type knife for cutting stencils

▷ Piece of glass for cutting base

▷ 1 (No. 4) stiff, round stencil brush

▷ Vivid lime green acrylic paint

▷ Cadmium red light acrylic paint

▷ Cerulean blue acrylic paint

▷ Raw sienna acrylic paint

Cutting and Piecing

All fabric must be washed and ironed. Trim selvage edges.

Cut forty 5″-square blocks from the tan outing-flannel bed sheet.

Cut forty 5″-square blocks from the green-and-tan plaid flannel. Use only the "heart" of the plaid design (see the photo) so all blocks are the same.

Stitch all blocks together, alternating plain blocks and plaid blocks in a checkerboard fashion, as shown in the photo. Piece eight blocks across and ten blocks down.

Cut two 4½″ x 44½″ strips and two 4½″ x 45½″ strips from the tan outing flannel to make a border around the blocks. Stitch in place.

Cut two 5½″ x 54½″ strips and two 5½″ x 53½″ strips from the green-and-tan plaid fabric to make the outer border. Stitch in place.

Trace each of the three Peter Rabbit patterns on the following page on a separate sheet of Mylar. Cut the stencils on the glass.

Use masking tape to block out parts of the stencils that will be painted with different colors. Paint the rabbits, referring to the photo for placement and color.

Using a black laundry marker, outline the different parts of the stencils with dotted lines. Draw in eyes, noses, and whiskers. Practice drawing on several sample rabbits on scrap fabric.

Allow the paint to dry overnight, and set with a hot, dry iron. Use a pressing cloth to avoid scorching.

Assembling and Finishing

Layer the backing, batting, and top. Baste together.

Quilt along all seams.

Add a 1″ tie of yarn in the center of each green-and-tan plaid block.

To finish the edges, bring the backing material and batting to the front of the quilt. Fold under to make a 1″ hem, and pin. Hem to the quilt top. ♡

WHIRL OF MAPLE LEAVES
(color plate 31)

Intermediate

Patchwork Quilt with Stenciled Blocks
52" x 69"

Materials

▷ 5 yards of 36"-wide unbleached muslin for quilt-top blocks, border, and backing

▷ 3 yards of 36"-wide dark green cotton fabric for quilt-top blocks and borders

▷ Quilt batting, twin size

▷ ¼ (3½ oz.) skein each of 4-ply dark green and bright red wool yarn

▷ 1 (12"-square) sheet of frosted Mylar

▷ X-acto-type knife for cutting stencils

▷ Piece of glass for cutting base

▷ 1 (No. 4) stiff, round stencil brush

▷ Hooker's green acrylic paint

▷ Cadmium red light acrylic paint

▷ Yellow oxide acrylic paint

Cutting and Piecing

All fabric must be washed and ironed. Trim selvage edges.

Cut six 12½"-square blocks from the muslin. These blocks will be set together with nine-patch blocks and arranged diagonally on the quilt top.

To make twelve nine-patch blocks, cut twelve 4½"-square blocks from the unbleached muslin and ninety-six 4½"-square blocks from the dark green fabric. Piece each nine-patch block from eight green squares and one muslin square, placing the muslin square in the center of the nine-patch. Two of these nine-patch blocks will be used full size.

To make six triangular pieces from six nine-patch blocks, draw a diagonal line across the center of a block, add a ¼" seam allowance along the diagonal, and cut; discard the smaller piece. Repeat with five blocks.

To make four small triangular pieces from four nine-patch blocks, draw an X from corner to corner across a block, dividing it in quarters. Add a ¼" seam allowance on two sides of one quarter, and cut; discard the remaining piece. Repeat with three blocks.

Set the large unbleached muslin blocks and the full-size

nine-patch blocks together, alternating them in a checkerboard fashion, as shown in the layout. Piece two large unbleached muslin blocks across and three large unbleached muslin blocks down, and fit the large triangular pieces around the edges and the small triangular pieces in the corners.

Cut two 1½" x 36½" strips and two 1½" x 51½" strips from the dark green fabric to make a border around the blocks. Stitch in place.

Cut two 4" x 43½" strips and two 4" x 53½" strips from the unbleached muslin to form a second border. Stitch in place.

Cut two 6" x 54½" strips and two 6" x 60½" strips from the dark green fabric to form a third border. Stitch in place.

Place the Mylar on the maple leaf pattern on the following page, and trace. Cut the stencil on the glass.

Use masking tape to block out parts of the stencil that will be painted with different colors. Paint the dark green leaves first, then all the red hearts, and last, the maple leaves. Paint the leaves by blending red, yellow, and green paint. Practice on a scrap of fabric before painting the quilt top.

Allow the paint to dry overnight, and set with a hot, dry iron. Use a pressing cloth to avoid scorching.

quilt-top layout

Assembling and Finishing

Layer the backing, batting, and top. Baste together.

Tie off the quilt with 1" ties, using the red and green yarns together. Place the ties as shown in the color plate.

To finish the edges, bring the backing material and batting to the front side. Fold under to make a 1" hem, and pin. Hem to the quilt top. ♡

TRUE OAK LEAVES
(color plate 32)

Patchwork Quilt with Stenciled Blocks
56″ x 84″

Materials

▷ 1 twin-size light peach polyester/cotton–blend bed sheet for quilt-top blocks and border

▷ 1 twin-size dark brown polyester/cotton–blend bed sheet for quilt-top blocks

▷ 5 yards of 36″-wide unbleached muslin for quilt backing

▷ Quilt batting, twin size

▷ 1 (7″-square) sheet of frosted Mylar

▷ 1 (5″ x 9″) sheet of frosted Mylar

▷ X-acto-type knife for cutting stencils

▷ Piece of glass for cutting base

▷ 1 (No. 4) stiff, round stencil brush

▷ Burnt sienna acrylic paint

▷ White acrylic paint to mix with the burnt sienna

Cutting and Piecing

All fabric must be washed and ironed. Trim selvage edges.

Cut thirty-nine 7½″-square blocks from the light peach fabric.

Cut thirty-eight 7½″-square blocks from the dark brown fabric.

Piece the blocks together, starting with a peach-colored block and alternating colors in a checkerboard fashion (see the color plate). Piece seven blocks across and eleven blocks down.

Cut two 5″ x 58½″ strips and two 5″ x 77½″ strips from the peach fabric to form a border. Stitch in place. Press all seams onto the brown fabric.

Place the 7″-square sheet of Mylar over the large oak leaf pattern on the following page, and trace. Trace the small oak leaf pattern on the 5″ x 9″ sheet of Mylar. Cut the stencils on the glass.

Paint the large oak leaves with burnt sienna on the peach blocks, as shown in the photo. For the small oak leaves, mix the white paint with the burnt sienna paint. Stencil the small oak leaves on the dark brown blocks. As stenciling proceeds, the pattern will create a circle of leaves on each block (see the photo). The dark brown fabric absorbs the paint, so it may be necessary to paint the small leaves a second time.

Allow the paint to dry overnight, and set with a hot, dry iron. Use a pressing cloth to avoid scorching.

Assembling and Finishing

Using a No. 3 (hard) lead pencil or dressmaker's marking pencil, draw a 6″ circle around each of the large oak leaves. Tracing around a salad plate works well. Add half-circle quilting lines on the border, using the same 6″ circle template.

Layer the backing, batting, and top. Baste together.

Quilt along all seams, and quilt the penciled-in circles. Quilt a second set of circles by quilting through the center of the leaves in each circle of small oak leaves.

To finish the edges, bring the quilt-top fabric and the batting to the back side of the quilt. Fold under to make a 1″ hem, and pin. Hem to the backing. ♡

PINEAPPLE

(color plate 33)

Intermediate

Patchwork Quilt with Stenciled Blocks

60½″ x 73″

Materials

▷ 2 twin-size white polyester/cotton–blend bed sheets for the quilt-top blocks and backing

▷ 2 yards of 36″-wide green calico print for mullions and border

▷ Quilt batting, twin size

▷ 1 (7″ x 9″) sheet of frosted Mylar

▷ X-acto-type knife for cutting stencils

▷ Piece of glass for cutting base

▷ 1 (No. 4) stiff, round stencil brush

▷ Cadmium yellow light acrylic paint

▷ Yellow oxide acrylic paint

▷ Chromium oxide green acrylic paint

Cutting and Piecing

All fabric must be washed and ironed. Trim selvage edges.

Enlarge the tumbler diagram on the following page, and cut 64 tumbler-shaped blocks from the white fabric.

Using the same tumbler diagram, make a half-tumbler pattern by enlarging the diagram, drawing a line down the center, and adding a ¼″ seam allowance along the center line. Using this pattern, cut 16 half-tumbler blocks from the white fabric.

Cut seventy-two 1½″ x 10″ strips and seven 1½″ x 60″ strips from the green calico print to form mullion strips around the tumbler blocks.

Piece nine short mullion strips to the slanting sides of ten tumbler blocks, making a horizontal row with eight full blocks and one half-tumbler block at each end. Repeat with the remaining blocks, making seven more rows. Piece the eight rows together with the seven long mullion strips.

Cut two 2½″ x 64″ strips and two 2½″ x 71½″ strips from the green calico for a border. Stitch in place.

Place the Mylar on the pineapple pattern on the next page, and trace. Cut the stencil on the glass.

Use masking tape to block out parts of the stencil that will be painted with different colors (see the photo). Place the stencil on the blocks so that the wide part of the pineapple fits the wide part of the tumbler block. Paint every other block in a checkerboard fashion, as shown in the layout.

Allow the paint to dry overnight, and set with a hot, dry iron. Use a pressing cloth to avoid scorching.

quilt-top layout

Assembling and Finishing

Place the pineapple stencil upside down on the unpainted blocks, and mark the design on the fabric, using a No. 3 (hard) lead pencil or dressmaker's marking pencil.

Layer the backing, batting, and top. Baste together.

Outline quilt all parts of the stenciled design. Quilt all penciled-in lines and along all seams.

To finish the edges, bring the quilt-top border and batting to the back side of the quilt. Fold under to make a 1″ hem, and pin. Hem to the backing. ♡

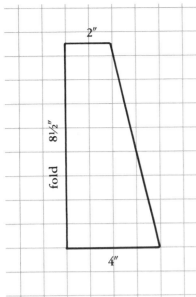

tumbler diagram
1 square = 1 inch

THEOREM THEME
(color plate 34)

Whole-Cloth Quilt with Appliqué and Stenciled Design
62½″ x 89½″

Materials

▷ 2 twin-size pale yellow polyester/cotton–blend bed sheets for quilt top and backing

▷ 1 twin-size yellow-and-green striped polyester/cotton–blend bed sheet for appliqué strips and border

▷ Quilt batting, twin size

▷ 4 (14″ x 16″) sheets of frosted Mylar for theorem painting

▷ 1 (6″ x 14″) sheet of frosted Mylar for border stencil

▷ X-acto-type knife for cutting stencils

▷ Piece of glass for cutting base

▷ 1 (No. 4) stiff, round stencil brush

▷ Vivid lime green acrylic paint

▷ Hooker's green acrylic paint

▷ Cadmium red medium acrylic paint

▷ Burnt sienna acrylic paint

▷ Burnt umber acrylic paint

▷ Yellow oxide acrylic paint, or any color that harmonizes with color scheme

Cutting and Piecing

All fabric must be washed and ironed. Trim selvage edges. Make sure the top and bottom of the quilt-

top sheet are perfectly square to the sides; trim top and bottom if necessary.

Fold quilt top into quarters, matching corners. Press folded edges with a warm iron. These crease lines will act as guidelines for positioning the appliqué strips and stencil designs. Make the lines accurate.

Cut two 3½″ x 20″ strips and two 3½″ x 24″ strips from the striped fabric (following the stripes on the fabric) to make a picture frame measuring 11½″ x 15½″ (inside measurements). Miter the corners, matching stripes (see the diagram on page 52). Turn under ¼″ seam on all sides, and press.

Pin the frame in the center of the quilt top (see the photo), using the crease lines for a guide. Topstitch by machine, using matching thread.

Measure 4″ from the outside of the picture frame, and mark a line around the entire frame, using a No. 3 (hard) lead pencil or dressmaker's marking pencil.

Cut two 3½″ x 34″ strips and two 3½″ x 38″ strips from the striped fabric to make a second picture frame measuring 25½″ x 29½″ (inside). Make this frame in the same manner as the first frame. Position the second frame outside the first frame, using the crease lines for a guide, and stitch in place.

Mark a light pencil line 5″ above this second frame, measuring from its top edge. Mark a second light pencil line 5″ below the frame, measuring from its bottom edge.

Cut four 3½″ x 13″ strips and four 3½″ x 38″ strips

from the striped fabric to make two picture frames that measure 4½" x 29½" (inside). Position both frames as shown in the photo, using the pencil lines and crease lines for guides. Stitch in place.

Mark a line around the frames for an outer striped border by measuring 5" above the top edge of the top frame, 5" below the bottom edge of the bottom frame, and 5" from the left and right edges of all the frames.

Cut two 3½" x 61" strips and two 3½" x 88" strips from the striped fabric, following the stripes on the fabric, to make the border. Stitch in place as shown in the photo.

Cut two 2½" x 65" strips and two 2½" x 88" strips from the striped fabric to make the final border. Stitch in place.

Place one large sheet of Mylar on the theorem-painting stencil pattern on the following pages, and trace just the light green parts of the design (refer to the photo and color key). On the three remaining large sheets of Mylar, make separate stencils for the dark green parts; the reds, including oranges; and the browns, including golds. Use the small sheet of Mylar for the grape-leaf border (see page 136 in the Portfolio section). Omit the bunches of grapes to simplify the design. Cut the stencils on the glass.

When painting the theorem stencil, refer to the photograph. Always start with a light touch of paint and work it in darker for the shaded areas. Don't be timid about mixing colors. It may be wise to practice first on a scrap of fabric.

Paint the grape-leaf border with the Hooker's green paint, referring to the photo for placement of the border stencils.

Allow the paint to dry overnight, and set with a hot, dry iron. Use a pressing cloth to avoid scorching.

Assembling and Finishing

Using a No. 3 (hard) lead pencil or dressmaker's marking pencil, mark quilting lines on the background outside the picture frames. The diamond pattern shown in the photo works well.

Liberties can be taken with a black laundry marker for adding accents on the strawberry and watermelon seeds and for drawing small, broken outlines where stenciled parts need to be emphasized. Study the color photo to determine where these lines should go. Don't overdo it, though. Practice using the marker on a piece of scrap fabric before decorating the quilt-top design.

Layer the backing, batting, and top. Baste together.

Quilt around all parts of the stenciled theorem painting. Quilt along the seams around all frames and borders. Quilt the penciled-in background lines and the stems on the grape-leaf border.

To finish the edges, bring the quilt-top fabric and batting to the back side of the quilt. Turn under to make a 1" hem, and pin. Hem to the backing. ♡

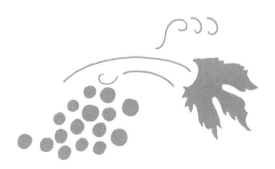

(turn page for full-size stencil pattern)

Color Key:

1 = bright red
2 = dark green
3 = medium brown
4 = gold
5 = orange
6 = dark red
7 = light green
8 = bright lime green

118

"The doing of a little thing well prepares for doing a bigger thing better."

— *Unknown*

120

PART FOUR

The Smaller Project

Looking for a stencil project other than a quilt? Many interesting projects — wall stencils, a stenciled floor and floorcloths, a bib, a log carrier, and others — are shown in the color photos of the quilts. Instructions for most of these projects follow. But there's no limit to what or where you can stencil — simply adapt these guidelines to the project of your choice. ♡

Early American Wall Stencil

(color plate 1, Wild Rose quilt)

The Early American stencil design seen on the wall bordering the window casing is attributed to Moses Eaton, Jr., of Hancock and Dublin, New Hampshire. This stencil pattern was discovered in a house built in 1804 by Governor Benjamin Pierce of Hillsborough, New Hampshire. A faithful interpretation of the stencil pattern can be found on page 138 (center) in the Portfolio section.

Procedures for wall stenciling can be adapted from the general rules for stenciling on fabric. When cutting a Mylar stencil for walls, leave an extra-wide border at the top of the stencil to act as a guide in positioning the stencil against the ceiling or window casing. When painting, tape the stencil to the wall with masking tape.

Either acrylic or latex paint can be used for wall stenciling. Flat or semigloss paints used for painting walls and woodwork also work well.

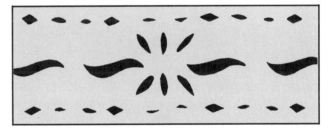

Use only a little paint on the stencil brush to prevent dripping and to make it easier to control the paint. Paint the stencil until the color reaches the desired darkness. This does not necessarily mean adding more paint to the brush — darken the color by using up the sparse amount of paint left on the brush.

Of course, a freshly painted wall is most worthy of the stencil efforts of an artist. ♡

Stenciled Floor

(color plate 6, Country Chickens quilt)

The stenciled floor shown in this barn is painted from the same grape-leaf stencil pattern as the border design of the Theorem Theme quilt. The pattern can be found on page 136 in the Portfolio section.

The floor must be prepared with a fresh coat of latex or oil-based paint before the stenciling can take place. Allow the floor paint to dry thoroughly before stenciling it, and let the stenciled floor cure-dry for several days before applying several finish coats of polyurethane to the entire floor. Satin polyurethane makes a nice finish. ♡

Canvas Floorcloths

(color plate 8, Whig Rose quilt
color plate 27, Oak Leaf and Reel quilt)

The small stenciled canvas floorcloth shown in color plate 8 uses the same design as the Whig Rose quilt, and the floorcloth in color plate 27 uses the stencil pattern of the Oak Leaf and Reel quilt.

Floorcloths are made from heavy awning canvas. If you wish, you can hem the edges by machine, using a zigzag stitch and a heavy-duty needle. Both sides of the canvas must be coated with several base coats of paint. Water-based acrylic or latex paints will cause shrinkage of about an inch per yard. If that's a problem, it can be eliminated by using oil-based paint. Paint the stencil design over the base coats; one stenciling of acrylic paint should be sufficient. Cover the stenciled floorcloth with several layers of polyurethane. Allow each coat of paint

Whig Rose floorcloth

or polyurethane to dry thoroughly before proceeding with subsequent coats.

When properly painted, floorcloths last for many years, even when used in areas of heavy traffic. To protect a finished floorcloth from damage, be sure to keep it flat on the floor, using masking tape to secure the corners to the floor. Floorcloths can be cleaned and cared for in the same way as a linoleum floor. ♡

Oak Leaf and Reel floorcloth

Baby's Bib

(color plate 9, Teddy Bear quilt)

A baby's bib can be constructed in three layers much like a quilt. This bib is made from two 8″ squares of muslin and a thin layer of polyester-fiber batting, all cut to the shape of the bib pattern.

Make the bib pattern by enlarging the diagram below. Cut the backing fabric, polyester batting, and top fabric from the pattern. Stencil paint the Teddy Bear design on the top fabric, following the stenciling instructions for the Teddy Bear quilt (see page 66). Layer the three pieces together, and pin. Bind the edges with bias tape, and attach two 14″-long bias-tape ties at the neck edge. Outline quilt all parts of the stenciled design.

Because the bib will be washed many times, it's best to apply the stencil paint heavily. Extra care in setting the paint will also prolong a fresh appearance. Do not wash with bleach. ♡

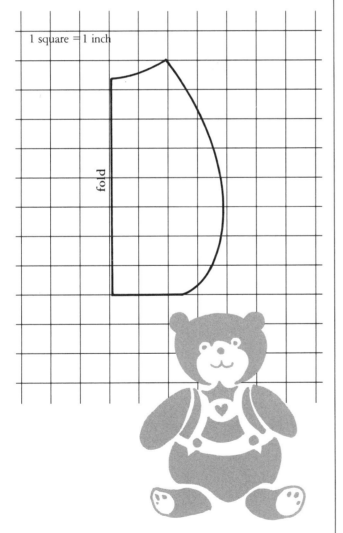

1 square = 1 inch

fold

Canvas Log Carrier

(color plate 10, Holly Wreath quilt)

The canvas log carrier hanging on the door handle is stenciled with the same design as the Song Birds quilt (see page 81). To make this sturdy log carrier, you'll need a 20″ x 36″ piece of heavy awning canvas and two 2″ x 24″ strips of canvas. Fold under a ½″ hem on all sides of the rectangular piece of canvas. Pin, press, and machine stitch with a heavy-duty needle. Measure 7″ on both sides of all four corners, and fold down each corner to form a triangle. Pin the triangles in place, press, and stitch.

To make the handles, fold the 2″ strips of canvas in half lengthwise, press the raw edges under, and top-stitch close to the edges. To attach the handles to the carrier, place the ends at the bottom edge of the 7″ triangles, using one strip for each side of the carrier (see the diagram). Stitch the handles along the full 7″. The stencil design should be painted after the carrier is completed.

A log carrier makes a welcome Christmas gift. Paint the Song Bird stencil pattern a bright red, add a dash of black on the wing, leg, and eye, and add a bright yellow bill. Stencil a little red topknot, and you've created a cardinal. Garnish with a green sprig of holly, taken from the Holly Wreath quilt pattern (see page 69). It's a gift that will be long remembered and appreciated. ♡

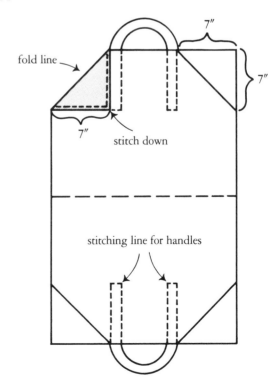

fold line

stitch down

7″

7″

7″

stitching line for handles

Upholstered Chair Fabric, Stenciled Fireplace Screen

(color plate 12, Leaf and Chain quilt)

The chair in this photo is upholstered with a fabric stenciled with a design much like that of the Leaf and Chain quilt. A sturdy "weaver's" fabric was chosen, and the design was stenciled over the entire fabric before upholstering. The paint was set with a hot iron before the fabric was cut and stitched to fit the cushions.

The fireplace screen is constructed from old 5″-wide painted boards that are well weathered. The flower-filled compote is made up of assorted stencils; some can be found on pages 128 and 137 in the Portfolio section, and others are borrowed from various stencil patterns used for the quilts. Rub the newly painted stencils with a metal pot scrubber to give the screen an antique look.

The diagram below for the fireplace screen produces a symmetrical design. But the design need not be such — have fun by making your own arrangement. Use different parts of the quilt stencil patterns and other patterns found in the Portfolio section. ♡

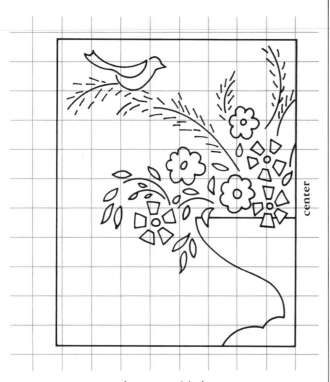

1 square = 1 inch

Canvas Table Cover

(color plate 16, Song Birds quilt)

On the chest of drawers is a small table cover made of canvas. To make the cover, follow the instructions for making the floorcloth discussed earlier. The stencil pattern used for this floorcloth is the same pattern used for the Creeping Periwinkle quilt (see page 89). ♡

Flannel Pillow

(color plate 30, Peter Rabbit quilt)

The soft outing-flannel pillow matches the Peter Rabbit quilt and was made of scraps left over from the quilt. The shape of the scraps dictated the design of the pillow top. The rabbit stencils were painted after the pillow top was made, and the paint was set with a hot, dry iron. Stuffing the pillow was the final step.

If you make a stenciled quilt, you will surely want to make a pillow for an added accent. The quilt stencil patterns that fit a 12″ block make lovely stenciled tops for pillows. You'll need two 15″ squares of a fabric of your choice and a bag of polyester batting for the stuffing. Stencil the top before you assemble the pillow, following the general instructions for stenciling on fabric. The stenciled design can be outline quilted before the pillow is assembled by basting a thin layer of batting to the underside of the pillow top and then quilting. ♡

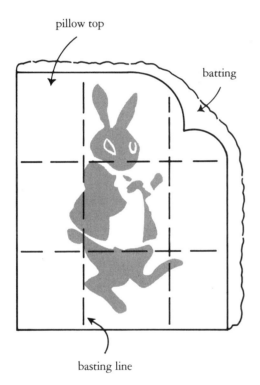

pillow top

batting

basting line

Theorem Painting, Tote Bag

(color plate 34, Theorem Theme quilt)

On the artist's easel is a theorem painting done on velvet fabric that's tacked over a canvas stretcher and slipped into a handmade box frame. The painting was stenciled from the same stencil pattern as the painting in the Theorem Theme quilt (see pages 118 and 119).

The canvas tote bag, hanging from the easel, repeats the same grape-leaf border design as used on the Theorem Theme quilt (see page 136, right, in the Portfolio section). The addition of the clusters of grapes creates a spot of color. Use a paper punch to cut the grapes in the stencil material.

A 16″ x 36″ piece of heavy artist's canvas and two 2″ x 16″ canvas strips are needed to make the tote bag (see the diagram below). Fold the large piece of canvas in half, forming a tube. Using a sewing machine with a heavy-duty needle, join the two 16″ sides by stitching a ¼″ seam. Stitch a ¼″ seam along the bottom of the bag. Turn under a 1″ hem at the top of the bag, press, and stitch.

On the outside of the bag, press a crease line on the front and back 2¼″ up from the bottom seam. Turn up 2″ on each end of the bottom seam, forming a triangle on each side. Pin and stitch in place. Coming up from the bottom corners of the triangles, press vertical crease lines to form the four corners of the bag. Stitch all pressed crease lines ¹⁄₁₆″ from the edges, giving the bag the shape of a grocery store sack. Fold the handle strips in half lengthwise, turn under the edges, press, and stitch close to both outer edges. Attach the handles at the top of the bag near the four corners. If you wish, add a colorful fabric lining of your choice. The stencil design should be painted with acrylic paint when the bag is completed. ♡

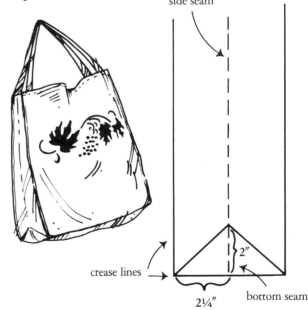

side seam

crease lines

2″

bottom seam

2¼″

"Creativity is practiced in a timeless realm and resembles play."
— *Joseph Ferguson*

PART FIVE

The Portfolio

All the stencil patterns in this portfolio are intended for making a stenciled quilt of your own design or for creating any other stencil project you might devise. Many combinations of patterns can be employed to develop a design that can be called your own. Planning a color scheme that harmonizes with your own decor will also give a brand-new feeling to these stencil patterns.

Many of the patterns reproduced in this section are appropriate for stenciling walls, furniture, floorcloths, wall hangings, and quilts. Border, frieze, medallion, and pieced and appliqué quilt designs resembling those of early America are included. Every stencil pattern in this portfolio is an original design or a faithful interpretation of an Early American design created by the author. ♡

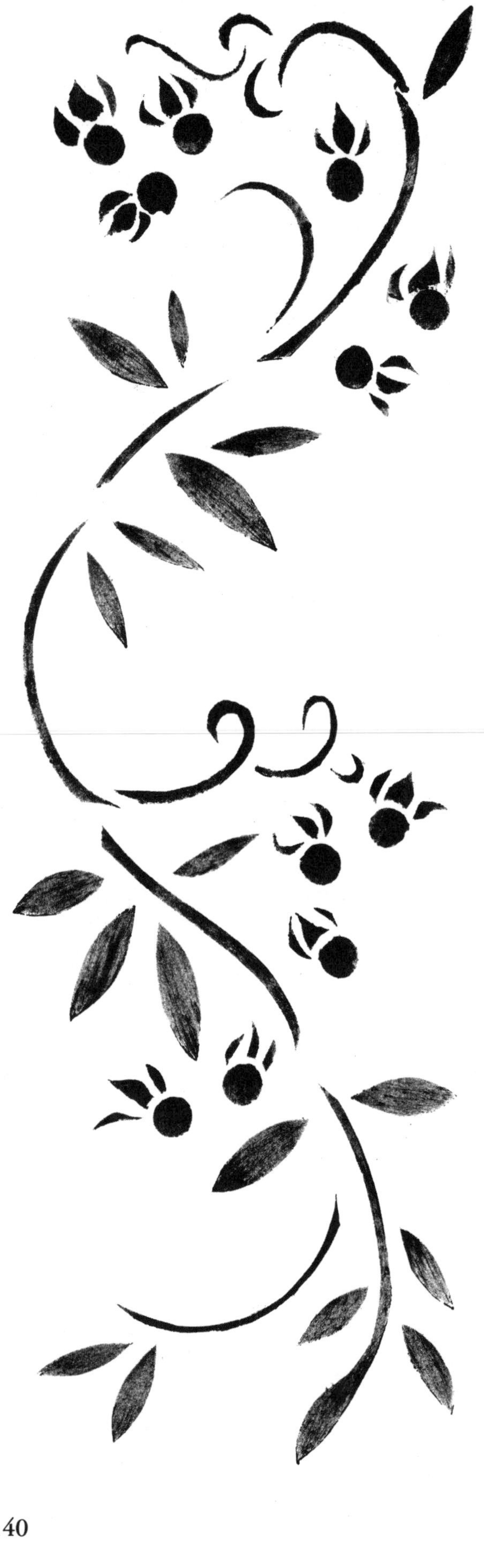

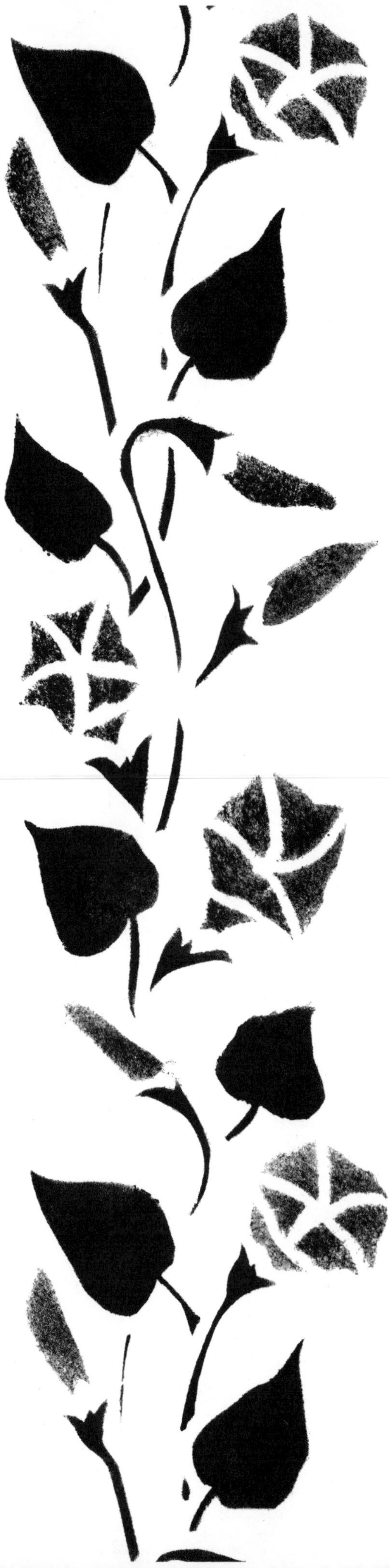

143

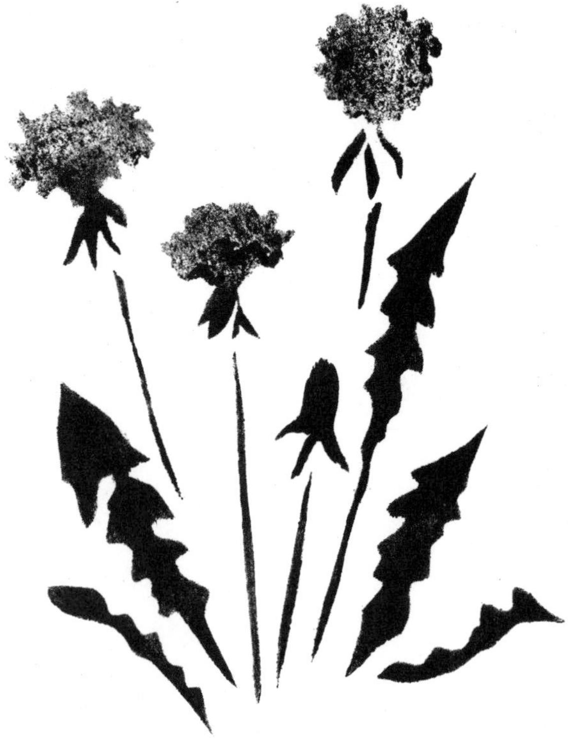

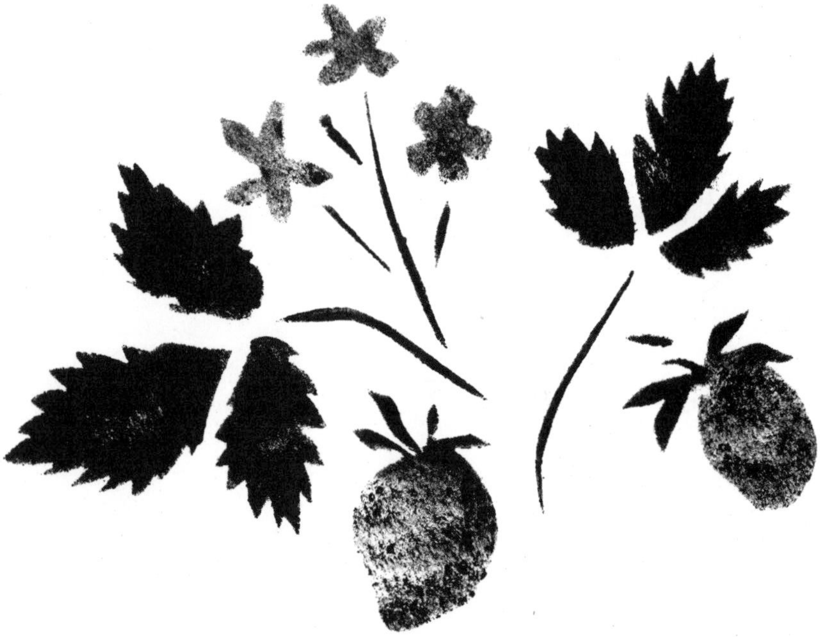

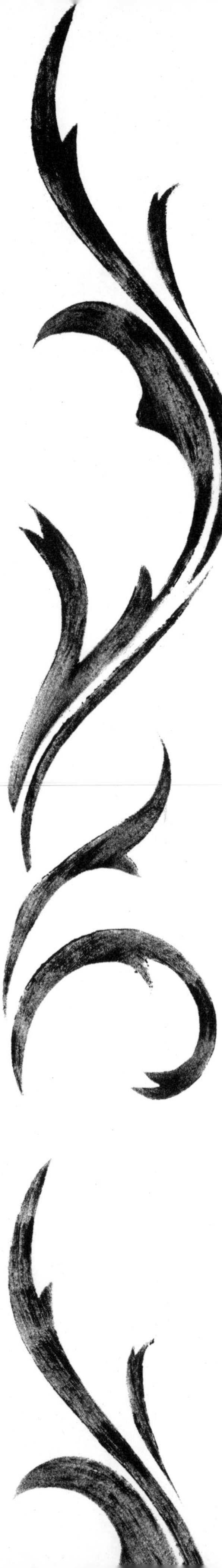

Resources

Books

Most of the following books are available from the publishers or can be ordered through a local bookstore. Check your library for volumes that are now out of print.

Better Homes and Gardens, eds. *Better Homes and Gardens American Patchwork and Quilting.* Des Moines, IA: Meredith Corp., 1985.

Bishop, Adele, and Cile Lord. *The Art of Decorative Stenciling.* rev. ed. New York: Penguin Books, Inc., 1985.

Golden, Mary. *The Friendship Quilt Book.* Dublin, NH: Yankee Books, 1985.

Higgins, Muriel. *New Designs for Machine Patchwork.* London: B. J. Batsford Ltd., 1980.

Hinson, Dolores A. *A Quilter's Companion.* New York: Arco Publishing, Inc., 1978.

McKim, Ruby S. *101 Patchwork Patterns.* rev. ed. New York: Dover Publications, Inc., 1962.

Rubi, Christian. *Cut Paper Silhouettes and Stencils.* New York: Van Nostrand Reinhold Co., 1972 (out of print).

Safford, Carleton L., and Robert Bishop. *America's Quilts and Coverlets.* New York: E. P. Dutton Co., 1980.

Slayton, Mariette Paine. *Early American Decorating Techniques.* New York: Collier Books, 1972 (out of print).

Waring, Janet. *Early American Stencils on Walls and Furniture.* New York: Dover Publications, Inc., 1937.

Mail-Order Suppliers

All of these companies sell printed or precut stencils, and many also sell their own brands of paints and other stenciling supplies.

Adele Bishop, Inc.
P.O. Box 3349
Kinston, NC 28502-3349
(Fabric paints and Japan paints; free brochure)

Avery-Morgan Ltd.
New England Stencil Co.
P.O. Box 253
Old Mystic, CT 06372
(Fab-Tex water-based paints)

Clotilde, Inc.
237 S.W. 28th St.
Fort Lauderdale, FL 33315
(Easy Stencil Paints, in sets, for fabric and other surfaces; free catalog)

Eastern Craft Supply
P.O. Box 341, Dept. 68000
Wyckoff, NJ 07481
(Fabric painting kits with acrylic paint; catalog $1, refundable with first order)